BLIND SPOT

WHAT THE EYES DIDN'T SEE...

BLIND SPOT

WHAT THE EYES DIDN'T SEE...

VOL I

A collection of 16 life-changing stories
that can impact your life.

Compiled by Sonia Poleon
Foreword by Lisa Nichols

www.BlindSpotAnthology.com
Instagram: @BlindSpotAnthology
Twitter: @BlindSpotAnthol

Contents

Foreword by Lisa Nichols

I don't think I have ever met a person who stands with strength, substance, faith and conviction who hasn't gone through something.

Nor someone who hasn't had the mountain of horror, hurt or pain that they had to climb over, of forgiveness that they had to go around or of self-doubt that they haven't had to burst through.

Everyone I've known – from my grandmother, father, spiritual mentor, to some of my most powerful business advocates, life leaders and spiritual teachers – have had their mountains.

In this phenomenal book, *Blind Spot*, you will read amazing stories of 'Looking Both Ways', 'Diamond under Pressure', 'The Journey', you will read phenomenal stories called 'I want My Life Back', 'Eve's Story', 'Seeing the Unseen', 'Held Hostage' and 'The Power in Green Flowers'.

You will hear of stories of women who had to climb, go under, go around or burst through the mountain.

This is a book that reminds you that determination, resiliency and perseverance is yours to access, and that your strength, your gift and your conviction may come wrapped in sandpaper.

That gift – of resiliency, power or unwavering faith – may have come wrapped in a situation, circumstance or experience that you would never have asked for and yet because you've gone through it, you are a better person, you are a more powerful being, you are a soldier for possibility.

So as you read this book, I want you to tap into your own resiliency. As you share the stories and you find your likeness and see your differences between you and the authors, I want you to celebrate how far you have come. Celebrate how far you are going and those individual soldiers and gladiators who are on that journey with you.

I'm honoured to be a part of the tribe of women and men who are willing to see what the eyes may not see and do what average or ordinary people may not be willing to do so that we can experience the extraordinary life that we all deserve.

Lisa Nichols
Motivating the Masses Inc

Introduction

Surely you know by now that it is not easy being you. Many times we hear people say, "You should be you 100% of the time." Let's face it, you are best at being yourself.

There are times in life when we just wish we were someone else. We look at people and think how wonderful their lives are, and sometimes that is exactly how people see our life – through rose-coloured glasses – and this can be so far from the truth.

Would you really want to change your life for someone else's 'lovely' looking life when you don't really know what goes on in their head, heart and home? Of course not.

Many human beings have a sad story to tell, no matter where you come from. There are very few people in this world who have not been through hard times.

You only have to look at Princess Diana, once voted the most photographed and followed woman in the world. Married to a Prince and due to be the Queen of England, she was definitely the most envied woman – well sort of. Prince Charles was much older than her and, as I recall, Lady Diana Spencer got married in her prime at the tender age of 20, while Prince Charles was already 32.

The world was so excited for them both, but it wasn't long before the cracks started showing. As we now know, Prince

Charles wasn't in love with Princess Diana at all. He married her because she was good wife material and she didn't have any negative things attached to her name, which was good for the royals. They considered her worthy of marrying the Prince and, of course, being the mother of future heirs.

It wasn't long after that Princess Diana became lonely in her heart, longing for the man she loved and married. He was in love with someone else and this broke her.

Just in the same way we look at other people's lives and think it is all a bed of roses, others are looking at yours thinking the same.

It takes courage to speak out and share your inside story with the world. All the co-authors in this book have searched their inner selves and decided that no more can they hide what has been affecting them – it's time to speak out, spread the word, take a stand and stand up for what is right.

It takes an enormous amount of courage and determination to write about the things that have affected you and made a massive impact on your life, so I commend these authors and hope you, the reader, is able to find solace in each of their stories.

Everyone has a story and no two stories are exactly the same. There are similarities, but ultimately, there is always a twist that enables our stories to be unique.

No matter where in the world you come from – north, south, east or west – no two stories are exactly the same. This means you are unique and you should be proud of yourself.

The stories in this book cover a wide range of topics, including depression, low self-esteem, mental health, loneliness, death, near-death experiences, heartache, sibling rivalry, financial starvation, loss of a child and, of course, marital issues.

The *Blind Spot* collaboration was just as much for them as it is for you.

Those author whose goal was to become a published author, I congratulate you because you have come a long way. By sharing your story, you have become a better person, with a deeper and clearer understanding of who you are.

You were the keeper of your story and of your truth and you have chosen to share the truth with the world. For this, I thank you and give you the accolade that you so richly deserve. It is easy to decide to write, but it is harder to actually write about your story.

You could have decided to sing or speak about your story but instead, you decided to write about it. By writing, you have enabled others to be a part of your journey, opened up your heart, mind and bared your soul to allow them in.

Your story will paint a picture in their minds that only they can see. This is the beginning of the end of that section of pain, release it and let it go, for your future holds great things for you.

You have had an energy shift in your head and now it is time to share with the world what has been making you for all these years.

The authors in this book have written some inspiring, heart-touching stories that I know will encourage and empower you on your journey.

"Every successful person has a painful story and every painful story has a successful ending."

Anonymous

Ansa Archibong

www.financial-intelligence.co.uk
Twitter: Fin_Intelligence_UK
LinkedIn: Ansa Archibong

"Never take trust and instincts for granted."

Ansa started his accountancy career in the United Kingdom after graduating with a 2.1 in Accountancy and Finance from the University of West London.

He is a qualified accountant and has worked in both practice and private sectors for the micro, small and medium-sized markets, incorporating all disciplines from general practice management to finance systems implementation, asset management, tax advisory and outsourcing with the aid of cloud technology.

Prior to joining the accountancy profession, he attended the Maritime Academy of Nigeria, where he studied Marine Transportation and worked in the Nigerian shipping industry for a few years as a shipping executive.

He is the founder and CEO of Financial Intelligence, an accountancy firm based in London, that provides general accountancy and tax advisory services, specialising in risk management within the confines of financial due diligence.

Financial Intelligence is a practising member of the Association of Chartered Certified Accountants (ACCA), the International Federation of Accountants (IFAC) and regulated to undertake a range of credit-related activities under the Financial Services and Markets Act 2000 (FSMA).

Financial Due Diligence

As he stared through the walls of the aquarium, I could see the tears rolling down his cheeks. It was obvious he was in pain and I could understand such pain, as I was physically present when it all took place. It was something we never anticipated and it turned out to be a very important life lesson. I am quite pleased to share with the readers of this book, so that they may learn from our collective experience and apply this in their daily lives.

Ndidem, as he is known to most of his close friends and family, grew up very poor and was the first child of three siblings. He was raised by a single mother, Mma, who divorced his father, a chronic and extreme alcoholic. However, despite such mishaps occurring in her brief and painful married life, his mother managed to focus on raising her son to become a great man, role model and contributor to society.

Mma never attended school or college and therefore had no formal education, but was a great indigenous farmer and business woman. Despite her inability to read, she managed to acquire land, which was cultivated over the years and produced a substantial harvest year on year, paving the way to sell her produce to the local market at an exorbitant profit.

The net proceeds from dealings with the local market in several villages equipped her with the resources to raise her three children to the status of a marine navigator, insurance executive and computer scientist.

She really understood and appreciated the power and significance of education, despite her limitations, and was always willing to purchase school uniforms, books and shoes for Ndidem, who thus was able to pursue his goal of becoming a mariner.

Learning from his mother's personal experience and business struggles, Ndidem was extremely driven and excelled in all subjects during his years at college, and was also a great sportsman, leader and inspiration to his teammates. He was well respected by his teachers and among his peers, and worked extremely hard to pass all his exams with flying colours.

Based on his outstanding success upon graduation and achieving top grades, he was able to secure a trainee clerk job with the Nigerian Ports Authority and later as a cadet on board one of the country's ocean-going vessels.

At the time, there were 21 ocean-going vessels wholly owned and controlled by the Nigerian National Shipping Line. This was the flagship of the nation, set up by the Nigerian Government in the 1950s to compete within the shipping industry with the major European lines.

Nigeria, a trading economy by virtue of its abundant natural resources, strategic and geographical location, is indisputably a maritime nation and therefore trades with several international countries.

A significant volume of the goods transported between all trading partners is done through shipping. Hence millions of cargoes were being shipped in and out of the country, contributing immensely to the country's GDP. As a result of the success of the Nigerian company, Ndidem and his teammates were paid handsomely for their hard work and commitment.

Based on the substantial monetary rewards associated with his career, he proposed to his childhood girlfriend and they tied the knot a year later. The joy of the arrival of their first child followed, then five more. Ndidem had always been a family man and cared very much about his partner, the love of his life.

During his tenure at the Nigerian National Shipping Line, Ndidem rose from the ranks of a deck cadet to chief officer/first mate. His high achieving and winning streak continued, so it was no surprise that, after the successful implementation and execution of several trading expeditions, he decided to study Marine Navigation at Plymouth University in the United Kingdom.

His admission to the university to pursue navigation and maritime science yet again brought so much pride and joy to his immediate and extended family. It became clear that he was making the right decisions, had the right attitude and Midas touch – anything he touched turned into gold.

As well as having to become a resident of the United Kingdom and raise a young family, no one knew what to expect from a non-African experience. But Ndidem understood that it created an opportunity for him to advance further in his studies and fulfil his dreams of becoming a qualified mariner.

With the support of his new family and self-determination, he continued to excel and outperform his colleagues, despite a few setbacks he faced as a foreigner. However, this was the fuel he needed to prove that he was an exceptional individual, which he demonstrated in the end.

Yet again, he proved he had the Midas touch and was constantly recognised for his outstanding academic achievements by both the university and the Nigerian Government, his current employer.

Upon successful completion of his education, he went back to sea as a chief officer on board several ocean-going vessels and, within seven months of returning from university in the United Kingdom, he was promoted to the position of a sea captain/master mariner in charge of an entire ship, responsible for the safety of the crew and the cargo pertaining to the national carrier.

Having graduated from a foreign university and become a master mariner, the world was his oyster. With his new status, wealth of knowledge and experience gained in the navigation field, Ndidem continued to deliver exceptional operational performance.

However, at some point in his career, he realised that his trips away from his family were not making him happy, as he could not travel all the time with them. So he decided to look into getting an onshore job that would enable him to maintain the same standard of living but still have a better quality of life with his family.

Several years down the line, Ndidem decided to quit the sea life and embark on a Master's degree programme at the World Maritime University in Malmo, Sweden. His choice of study was Maritime Safety and Environmental Administration, which again was within the confines of the shipping profession.

Ndidem excelled and graduated with a distinction. His sponsor, the Nigerian Government, kept track of their citizen's proud accomplishments. Based on his new-found qualification and wealth of experience, he was offered the position of assistant chief maritime surveyor at the Federal Ministry of Transport Marina, Lagos.

Lagos is the largest commercial city in Nigeria, a major financial centre in Africa and houses one of the largest and busiest ports on the African continent. But after a brief stint in Lagos, he was transferred to Federal Ministry of Transport in Warri, and promoted to chief maritime surveyor.

Warri, unlike Lagos, is seen as one of the major oil hubs of petroleum activities and businesses in South Nigeria. It is the commercial capital city of Delta state, with a population of about 500,000 people.

As a major oil hub, a lot of the cargo generated requires the use of river-going vessels to transport these products. However, to ensure the safety of the crew and cargo, the vessels needed to be seaworthy or else they would be deemed non-operational.

In Nigeria, there are a number of extremely corrupt individuals who have the power and influence and are also able to have the resources to own a number of vessels that would service the companies operating within the oil industry. The marine surveyor is similar to the role of a company auditor, reviewing a set of accounts prior to issuing a clean bill of health to investors, giving them assurance that the company in itself is worthy of further investments or has the potential to reward any risk taking investor.

The marine surveyor is the person who conducts inspections, surveys or examinations of marine vessels to assess, monitor and report on their condition and the products on them, as well as inspecting damage caused to both vessels and cargo. Marine surveyors also inspect equipment intended for new or existing vessels to ensure compliance with various standards or specifications.

It was therefore Ndidem's role, as the head of the Ministry of Transport, to ensure that any vessel operating in the coastal inland waterways is seaworthy and possesses a Certificate of Safety clearance from the Ministry.

Corruption is prevalent in many countries, but in Nigeria it is at astronomical proportions and continues to have a negative impact on society up until today. In Warri, a significant number of boat/ship owners had a substantial number of vessels operating the inland waterways, but these vessels were not seaworthy. However, these vessels still managed to obtain clearance from the Ministry of Transport by bribing government officials with vast sums of money in return for a clean bill of health.

During Ndidem's tenure at the ministry, he uncovered these very disturbing facts. The ship owners never cared about the safety of lives or goods being transported each day, but only cared about sustaining a business model that allowed them to maintain their lavish lifestyles.

Ndidem was ambitious and always wanted to be extremely successful, but he needed to do so the legal way without endangering the lives of those around him. He therefore decided to make changes during his tenure. These changes brought about rebellion from those who had benefitted from this corrupt system for many years. Several attempts were made by Ndidem to report his frustrations to his superiors and those in higher authorities, but such complaints fell on deaf ears, as they were all part of the corrupt regime.

With an undeniable feeling of frustration, despite several futile attempts to report such illegal practices to the higher authorities, he decided to resign from his position as chief maritime surveyor to set up his own company as a marine consultant and surveyor.

Setting up of his company in Warri gave him the freedom and drive to make the changes that he was meant to do while serving under the government. Lucrative contracts were awarded by both local and multinational companies operating within the oil sector who understood the importance of operating seaworthy vessels.

On many occasions, there were record numbers of deaths due to a combination of manned vessels by a significant number of unqualified staff and the operation of non-seaworthy vessels. This was a nightmare for several companies who needed a reliable service that met the needs of the marketplace without any fatalities.

So it was a great relief when Ndidem's company came into the marketplace as a formidable competitor, with the aim of meeting the needs of the consumers. He managed to reduce the number of deaths associated with the shipping industry.

Based on his new-found freedom, Ndidem was able to grow his company and invested in a significant number of projects such as barges, water tankers and speedboats. Each investment contributed to the local economy and locals were employed to work on several projects within the company.

Ndidem was a role model and was always being invited to grandiose occasions, which enabled him to make contacts both in and out of the shipping industry. This increased his network of friends and business contacts.

It was on one of those splendid occasions that he met Dr. Mike, who was introduced to him by the guest of honour. Dr. Mike was a very bright guy, impeccably dressed, with an academic background and had bagged a PhD in Applied Economics from the University of Pennsylvania in Wharton, United States of America. Although Ndidem did not understand the world of economics to that degree, he was impressed with the doctor's resume. They hit it off instantly, discussing issues affecting the economy and Nigeria's role in helping indigenous companies to create jobs for local people.

Dr. Mike said he had worked with several companies in Europe and the United States, but found that it was only in Nigeria he felt at home. This was no surprise, as this was his birthplace and he also felt that, despite his accomplishments, he needed to give back to his country and his fellow Nigerians by sharing his vast knowledge with society. It made perfect sense and this was the kind of person who shared the same philosophy of life as Ndidem.

Dr. Mike mentioned that he worked with the Nigerian Investment Promotion Commission in Abuja, the Federal Capital of Nigeria. He was also part of senior management that continues to advise the presidency on how to attract direct foreign investments into the country with the aim of reducing poverty and promoting economic development without any political attachment.

Ndidem was so impressed and proud of his new best friend's accomplishments that he introduced him to his wife, Eme, and their six children. Dr. Mike returned the favour on several occasions, bringing gifts for the children, as well as inviting Ndidem and his wife for dinner.

Business was looking good, demand for his company's services kept pouring in and Ndidem continued his winning streak. His passion to succeed never seemed to fade and his positive attitude allowed him to continue to expand his operations within the country.

Ndidem had also invited Dr. Mike to visit his office premises and he was impressed with the level of success he had attained. Ndidem never visited the office of Dr. Mike, even though he had his business card, as Mike was always in or out of the country on several world trips, aiming to promote the culture, image and hugely rewarding business environment to potential investors.

It was on one of his several visits to Ndidem's premises that Dr. Mike mentioned that they were looking to bring in foreign investors to invest in a major oil tanker operation. This oil tanker venture would be able to capitalise on the booming oil and gas industry, which would give each investor a substantial return on investment of US$35.5 million. This was valuable information and was made known mostly to the privileged few. Dr. Mike mentioned that the government would prefer to deal with foreign investors rather than Nigerians, as they could easily come up with the money.

However, an exception would be made to those who had no problems investing a minimum of $4.5 million in the project. The investor would make about eight times their money back within a short period of time. Dr. Mike also mentioned that the venture was of low risk, as this had the backing of the Nigerian government, which was keen to get this project off the ground and support all investors.

This made sense due to Nigeria's role in the oil and gas industry. Nigeria is a member of the OPEC group (Organisation of the Petroleum Exporting Countries) and the oil and gas sector accounts for about 35 per cent of gross domestic product, and petroleum exports revenue represents over 90 per cent of total exports revenue.

Upon receiving news of this deal, Ndidem decided to act on this, but first confided in his wife. Eme was uneasy at first and mentioned that, despite all the countless dinners, she had never met Mike's partner, love interest or any members of his family. Ndidem had explained that Mike was divorced in America and since then found it hard to settle down, even though he was deemed a suitor to numerous women. However, they both brushed aside his personal life and focused on the deal that would change their lives for the better.

Six days after speaking to Dr. Mike, Ndidem was able to contact all of his friends, acquaintances and the banks to raise the $4.5 million as requested. This was done over a 12-day period and the money was wired to a bank account provided by Mike.

Dr. Mike acknowledged receipt of the money through a telephone call to Ndidem and mentioned that he would embark on getting all the documentation approved by the Federal Government and have Ndidem introduced to the other foreign investors within two weeks.

Ndidem was so pleased that he would be able to embark on such a life-changing deal and even started making plans on how to expand his operations overseas. After two weeks, he tried to contact Dr. Mike to find out how he was getting on, but each time he called, his phone went to voicemail. He decided to leave a message asking Dr. Mike to get in touch with him and understood that perhaps he was working hard to get the contract secured.

After three weeks, there was no response from Dr. Mike. Ndidem got concerned and decided to visit his office premises in Abuja. He hoped that Dr. Mike had not fallen ill and hoped nothing terrible had happened to him while abroad. Dr. Mike had mentioned that he worked at the Nigerian Investment Promotion Commission and even handed out his business card to him when they first met at one of those impressive gatherings.

Upon his arrival in Abuja, Ndidem headed straight to the office premises and met with the receptionist. After exchanging pleasantries and handing over Dr. Mike's business card, Ndidem calmly stated the reason why he was visiting and asked to see Dr. Mike. The receptionist left her desk and went into another office, then asked Ndidem to go into the boardroom, accompanied by another gentleman.

He was asked to describe Dr. Mike. Ndidem was confused but he patiently described, in great detail, what Dr. Mike looked like. After giving the description, they told him the organisation had never employed or had any dealings with any Dr. Mike, and that none of their employees had attended the Wharton University of Pennsylvania. Ndidem was the victim of financial fraud.

Ndidem was speechless and in total shock. He realised that he had been duped. How could he explain this to his wife, family and friends? It was based on this sad development that he decided to sell his other investments just to repay all the loans to the banks and his friends.

Ndidem had lost everything he had worked so hard to build over the years. At an elderly age of 69, it was extremely painful and difficult having to start life all over again. Despite his wealth of business, technical knowledge and expertise in his chosen profession, he had no thought of conducting any financial due diligence. If this had been carried out, Ndidem would have identified all the red flags before going into any venture.

Life is full of dubious characters and there are many out there in the form of financial crooks who mean harm and have no conscience. Judging from this story, there was a great intent to cause harm. However, such risk can be prevented if you involve the services of an independent financial due diligence expert to investigate any potential business deal that is brought your way before committing your hard-earned capital. It is extremely difficult to build an empire, but very easy to destroy it.

If you find yourself in such a situation, remember that there are experts out there who are willing to help and guide you to see the wood for the trees in any situation. Financial Intelligence is one of those experts.

The acquisition of knowledge and engagement of an experienced and qualified accountant is never expensive in comparison to the cost of ignorance.

ClauDieon A Bowerbank

www.nova-solutions.co.uk
Email: claudb@nova-solutions.co.uk
Facebook: ClauDieon Bee
Twitter: @ClauDB14

"You See, How God Loves Me"

Married aged 22. Widowed aged 29.

ClauDieon naturally developed the chutzpah to raise two bereaved children in the dawning of the 21st century. Visually daunting to the onlooker, ClauDieon's tenacity to love her two children, while nurturing their minds to believe they're not simply a single-parent statistic, but instead, influential leaders in the making, has produced two focused university students.

ClauDieon's passion for singing has permitted her to perform across European platforms and internationally as a backing vocalist. Her love of literature and reading has consumed many of her 'free' hours.

She spent a number of years working as an outdoor clerk, attending court hearings with clients who faced similar situations she had endured, in litigation. Using her empathy, wisdom and negative experience of being in the court system, she empowered others to stand strong.

She is now finally coming into her own and is excited about her future, working towards new literary goals and waiting for her phone to ring with her next interview segment...

Look, Both Ways...

"Mummy, why is my Daddy's hand so cold? Mummy... "

Come on Cie, focus, you must focus – you 'must' focus. Yes, he has done the unthinkable in your mind, but she needs you. Tune in, listen and respond.

Isn't it funny how sometimes you have to instruct your brain to do the very thing that should be an automatic process? I was stuck – mentally stuck.

Hmm, it dawned on me, he didn't breathe out...

I inhaled deeply and released a breath, enough to fill two balloons in one breath. He didn't breathe out – could it be possible he's holding his breath? Maybe her touch will revive him and he'll let it out and smile at her to assuage the confusion on her little face, because right now – I don't know what to do, or say.

I tried my best to prepare them both when I arrived at my parents home and awoke them at 6am. I tried gently arousing them to ease them into a day that was far from serene. The next 18 hours proffered the gift of pain, which would alter their little lives, forever.

She tugged on my arm, which led me to look directly into her wide eyes. "Baby, Daddy's gone to rest in the clouds now, as he was in pain and very tired. Remember what mummy told you this morning?"

"But why didn't he say goodbye to me and MarShawn, Mummy?" she asked me in earnest.

Mia had always been the spokesperson for them both. She never spoke in the first person, they were always partnered, a team, a bond that I now realised would be the safety blanket they'd need to draw on in the days ahead.

"Daddy's last words were, 'Please tell Mia and MarShawn that I'll love them forever,'" I responded. In the same breath, he'd also admitted he wished he'd loved me better but knew, with God's help, I'd forgiven him and that I would continue to love him through the children.

"But Daddy always talks to us, and it's not fair that this time he just left. But it's okay, we'll go play in the garden and see if we can see him floating on a cloud."

"Okay Mia, that's a brilliant idea," I replied as I watched MarShawn just stand faithfully beside his sister, looking at his father's arm, which was as far as his height would permit.

"MarShawn, do you want to see Daddy's face?" As is MarShawn, he vehemently shook his head while his stare bore into my eyes, imploring me to make his young mind understand what was happening.

Mia worked her magic and said some exciting childlike comment to him. He raced out the door after her, focusing all his might on catching her up. They were aged four and six.

On cue, in came the undertakers to start preparing my husband, friend, mentor and wordsmith sparring partner... the words began falling over one another in my mind vying for first position of importance. I allowed them to do so as I looked on. They removed the bible I had placed under his crossed hands nine hours ago.

You see, I was the last person he saw on this earth before he inhaled for the last time. I was his songbird to transit him to his new journey. I knew I'd never sing those songs that I sang with such tenderness again. I didn't even recognise my voice, it was like I'd been endowed with a dual tone which caused me to read many emotions, but most significantly 'peacefulness' in the face of the man I'd known and loved since my early teens while comforting my own heart. There he lay, only permitted 29 years on this earth.

"'Til death us do part" had so become a reality in the fabric of my life, aged 29, a widowed mother of two beautiful but bereaved children who, I vowed to ensure, would live.

The body bag was brought outside, to a street lined three-persons deep. The silence was interrupted by a gut-wrenching moan. Someone's sorrow was being expressed, the moan guttural yet it could be felt as burning from the pit of one's stomach. I'd never experienced such grief, but it was like I was feeling that person's pain. The burning got worse, the sound got louder, I felt myself opening my mouth in sync with the pain bearer, "He's left me," she hollered while I lip synced the very same words... then blackness.

I had fainted, it wasn't me being empathic, it was I who moaned from the depths of my belly as the man I loved, fought, obeyed and bore children for was driven away in a black bag, in a black van, on a black day.

What did the future hold for us? Who would my children become as a young man and woman? These questions flew through my mind as I lay there, that was until someone had compassion on me and helped me up into a chair that was situated right there in the road.

Then my parents arrived and, as would be their stance in many days ahead, they took me to the car and expressed their condolences to the large grieving family. My father, who was a minister, switched into pastoral mode, ensuring all were in a stable enough state or had support, and they took us to collect the children, who had become overwhelmed with the sorrow that surrounded them. I nuzzled MarShawn's head under my chin and ensconced Mia to my side, using their body warmth to erase the coldness I could feel seeping around us.

Who would have known a surprise trip to see Beres Hammond in concert, one of Xavier's favourite artists, would result in the first signs of his illness manifesting on the fateful journey we took that day? And that the next 11 months of hospitals, treatments and tests would result in a day like today? God, I need you! I don't mean the clichéd prayer proffered in times of anguish, I REALLY need you because I can't allow anyone to see my distress that I have no clue of how I'm going to get through the days ahead. My worst fear has been realised today – I am going to be a single mother.

I always prayed from a little girl that I never wanted this to happen to me. I always prayed for a man to love me enough, to marry me and we would raise our children together, to the best of our ability with God at the centre of our family life. I promised to be the best wife he allowed me to be and every day of married life would be hailed as a blessing.

Two weeks, to the day... I can't believe a car hasn't been provided for the children and I. I sat there, driving in a car with Xavier's posterity, separated from the main family. How can this be? How can people find the capacity to permit their thought process to be so petty, at a time like this?

MarShawn and Mia chatted amongst themselves, looking so cute in their matching white Indian-style outfits. I didn't want them to be in black as it was too severe for their young lives. I wanted them to represent life, the future, posterity, and joy. I had to adorn myself in black, as it was a very black moment in the history of our lives, but it also marked the 'stubbornness' of black – the strength I would need to draw on in the coming days. The ink stain of the darkened sky that we know as night that cannot be removed until the sunrise highlights the time with its rays.

It was a day that I would need to remember, to ensure Mia and MarShawn are always reminded of the memorial. But in all other senses, I would work hard to eradicate the last 12 hours from my mind, my spirit and my heart. Why? To see a family who loved another human being to the extent that was portrayed today, but to see the very essence of the memories ignored, it is a day that could rob me of years of happiness and joy, so I choose to press 'delete'.

MarShawn and Mia ran around the house like runaway trains. It was the day to board the plane and the excitement in their faces filled the room. My mother had paid for us to get away to Florida for two weeks, just to grieve for a while and rest. It was just what we needed. The confusion, uncertainty and scariness of life – it was all there, suffocating me as I placed another item of clothing in our suitcase. I was struggling to breathe – death was sucking the life out of me and I was struggling to keep away from its vortex. I needed to have quiet time and plan for a future that was as uncertain as tomorrow.

Why didn't Phil and Trent say hello to me at the church? Why did Aunt Carrie insist on calling MarShawn by his father's name for the entire day? I wasn't mentioned in the funeral programme – why did cousin Nicki point that out to me? Why did my mother-in-law on the podium deliver a veiled threat? She'd looked so beautiful with her petite frame and high cheekbones, but as she spoke, her beauty dissipated before my very eyes. Why would you throw down a gauntlet at your son's funeral? Sometimes, just sometimes, ignorance was bliss.

We touched down in Miami, Florida, on the morning of September 11th. It was an eerie feeling, the roads were clear of traffic and people. We couldn't understand what was happening, but minutes before our arrival one of the worst tragedies to hit the USA had occurred – the destruction of the Twin Towers.

"Thank you Jesus for journeying mercies," I fervently whispered.

It was two weeks that we needed. I just allowed Mia and MarShawn to ask their questions, cry and play together, which in turn gave me time to process what had just happened in my life. But I wouldn't play back the day of the funeral in its entirety. That was too much pain to process right now. All I picked from the day to focus on was how handsome Xavier had looked in his white suit, and the bittersweet beauty of the children holding their red rose against their white outfits, waiting to drop it on their father's coffin to say goodbye.

We went sightseeing and to malls, but mainly stayed at the home of very good friends of my parents, who were pastors. They allowed us to stay by the pool most days and just be.

One thing that kept playing on my mind was the telephone call I received two weeks prior to my husband's death. It was from a work colleague who called to inform me that Xavier was rewriting his will. When I asked the reasons why, none was given. When I asked whether I needed to be present, I was told it was just a formality that I was informed.

Although the following two weeks were spent in some intimate and confessional moments with my husband, that caused me to feel very close to him. While he reassured me the children and I would be okay, something just wasn't sitting right with me.

I told the children we were going on an adventure to London for the day, under the guise of 'getting down to business'. It had been three months now, the children were attending one-on-one bereavement counselling sessions, and then we had family group therapy at Jigsaw4u, which are an amazing charity, where we met and solidified many friendships, both adult and children alike.

I had not heard from the executors of my husband's will and needed to do my own investigation, as they would not release a copy to me.

We walked over Waterloo Bridge, oooohing and aaaahing at the water and the huge glass buildings that lined the bank of the River Thames, which, in a child's eyes, are exciting and new. Funny thing is, every time I come to London, I have that feeling. If it's not the rich architectural history of Whitehall, then it's the delectables of Borough Market or the cultural enigma of Portobello Road and Camden Town.

"Mummy, where will our adventure take us now?" Mia asked, as her eyes shone with the innocence of all things new.

"Hmm, how about we walk to where they make television programmes? It's kind of magic," I replied, smiling at what their little minds would conjure up. Off we trotted to Bush House and I invented amazing stories that stretched their imagination and kept them amused.

We then stopped for lunch, because I knew within the next hour we'd have to be making our way home or I'd have to find a way to carry two tired children on the trains, which was no small feat.

We arrived at the Probate Registry. To the man in the street, it was just another building in the concrete corridor of High Holborn, but deep down I knew it held the key to my children's future. Yes, I was assured of my faith in God and that his promises to the widow and the fatherless were recorded numerous times in the Bible. But there was a level of fear that gripped my heart, as a mother, despite praying with the children that morning before we left home, asking God to allow us to have fun and for it to be a productive day in terms of my intentions.

I'd carried the relevant documents to obtain the paperwork I required. MarShawn and Mia went off to a bland-looking corner, with off-coloured beige carpet that had seen years of abuse from footsteps ingrained in its fibres. A corner that I knew they would both transform into something adventurous. It always fascinated me to watch them both at play; they could make the most sterile environment come alive with animation and childlike laughter that I always found therapeutic.

Mia's imagination would set the scene, while MarShawn soaked up her every word. But then it was like something ignited in him and he would spring to life inventing the characters. Within minutes, a full theatre performance was in motion, but the disagreement would come when MarShawn wanted to kill off Mia's character and she, with her spirit of resilience, would refuse to lay down and play dead, much to MarShawn's chagrin.

"Number 4629," a pretty elderly lady shouted out. Beautiful pale blue eyes were hidden behind a pair of glasses that had no place on such a delicate face – eyes that didn't match the bellowing tone she projected.

"How can I help you today Ma'am?" I knew it, her eyes belied her voice and now her mannerism confirmed the warmth I knew she possessed. But for some reason, it evoked an emotional response in me.

"I'm here to order a copy of my husband's will," I responded, with a voice that broke in places with emotion. Wow, that was actually hard to say.

The pregnant pause... hmm, this has happened before, I thought to myself. The bank when I notified them of Xavier's death, the Post Office, the children's school – in each case, once I started my business I had to give 'them' a moment to collect themselves, be it the removal of their glasses, the pitiful stare over the tops of their frames or the pause to look down at the paper for words that were not there and then speak – they all did it. It took them a moment to comprehend my life.

"I'm so sorry my love," she said as she looked over at the children and back at me.

"What was the date of death?"

"21 August 2001," I replied. Nearly three months to the day, I thought, as I stood there waiting for her as she shuffled off for some paperwork.

Hmm, time had flown... I had gone back to work about three weeks ago, but I was struggling. My poor work colleagues don't know whether to mention it or try to ignore it, and then others are trying so hard to be sensitive around me that it's a misfit. I'd been with this law firm for five years, so my family life was intricately woven into my work life – from the photos of my family on my desk, to the weekly accounts we all spoke about on a Monday of what had taken place over the weekend.

Thankfully, I only worked three nights a week, which equated to five full days of work – God, I'm grateful for your wisdom when I changed my work hours just under a year ago. Who would have known how beneficial this would be now I'm a single parent?

Aunty Lizzie was due home from South Africa any day now and promised to sit with the children one night a week to relieve mum and dad somewhat, which meant they would only need to sleep at my parents' home two nights a week now and be home five.

"Here we go, just fill in this form, sign right here and within 30 minutes, I'll process your request."

"Thank you," I said as I took the clipboard that would give me access to a document I should have received some weeks ago now, but hadn't.

I handed her back the form and she stepped away from the counter. I walked over to the children, trusting in their powers to spirit me away for the next 30 minutes into their world of endless possibilities and beauty.

She'd placed the document in an unsealed brown envelope. I thanked her for the service and took hold of the children. We crossed the main road and made the short walk to Lincoln Inn Fields, which had a place for the children to run around for a while before our journey home and provided me a brief moment to read Xavier's will.

"This is the Last Will and Testament of Xavier Nyle... "

My eyes blurred. I should have exercised my better judgement and read this when I was home.

I was paralysed with shock - God – Please - Help - Me!

Debbie Roberts

Email: DebbieRoberts2010@Gmail.com
Instagram: @Debbie_Dimples_Roberts
LinkedIn: Debbie Roberts

'Always Expect The Unexpected'

Born and raised in Brixton, south London, Debbie Roberts a mother of six, a dynamic woman and counsellor with a passion for seeing the youth aim for something positive in life. She is on a mission to change lives and impact the younger generations by taking them out of bad situations.

Through her organisation AIM HIGH, she's helped rehabilitated teenagers by giving them counsel and a sanctuary, free from the stereotypical youth culture of violence pervading the streets of London. As the saying goes, "where there is no vision the people perish."

The transformation in the lives of the youth provides the drive for this lifelong dedication.

Aim High

"Dickhead, dickhead, dickhead."

Imagine being called a dickhead by your own child, all because I refused to give him £6. I will never forget the word 'dickhead'. What do you say when you have a four-year-old and a two-year-old sitting down listening to a discussion that could have potentially gotten out of control?

"Okay," I said, "I am a dickhead."

"Mummy, LJ said that you're a dickhead. What's a dickhead?" Truth be known, I didn't know what to say, so I said,

"He didn't say 'dickhead' Olivia, he said 'pick head', and it's because of my hairstyle." She started to laugh and I pretended to laugh with her. My hair was in dreadlocks, so saying 'pick head' was all I could think of.

I was so angry. Dickhead – who does this 14-year-old boy think he is talking to? LJ had only been living back with us for one month and a week. He had just been suspended from school and was demanding that I still give him his daily allowance of £3 per day. "Hell no, I don't think so." The atmosphere in our home was unpleasant as a result of this.

In June 2010, I received a call from a private number. It was Kennington police station. They informed me LJ had been arrested and advised I needed to attend his interview before he could be considered for bail. POLICE, INTERVIEW,

BAIL, WHAT? His dad hadn't even said a word to me, despite him giving the police my telephone number 24 hours earlier. Nevertheless, what could I do besides be there for my son?

I had no idea that things had deteriorated between LJ and his dad, and I was shocked to find out he had been getting in trouble with the police.

Since LJ was a baby, he seemed to like being around older peers. He didn't gel well with children his own age. By the time he was five years old and had started school, he only played with older boys. He had no friends in his class, only in the classes above. I remember thinking all his family were older than him, so this is what he was used to.

By the time LJ was six years old, he had been excluded from school for disruptive behaviour. Every week there was a problem. I struggled to believe this, because at home LJ was the total opposite. My son was a polite, happy and funny boy.

I would say bye to him in the playground, but unknown to him, I would watch him from the classroom window. Barely 10 minutes into the lesson, he would be disruptive to the class. This was a daily occurrence. I even watched him throw cutlery around the dining room.

I tried everything with LJ. I punished him, as well as rewarding him, but the school complained every day. I had two children in the same school, LJ aged six and his older sister Lenni who was aged eight. Lenni was a star pupil, but the same could not be said for LJ. Due to LJ's continuous disruptive behaviour, I was faced with the dilemma of having a child who had no school to attend. I would regularly sit LJ down and talk with him. I asked LJ on more than one occasion why he was misbehaving. He always said he doesn't know why! That was, until the day LJ was permanently excluded from school.

"I do it because I want to live with my dad!" LJ said. In amazement, I asked LJ to repeat himself. LJ confidently looked at me and said, "I want my dad, Mum."

What was I supposed to do now? I had two children who had no relationship with their dad. I had no idea where he lived. I decided to look for where he stayed, because he never answered my phone calls.

Their dad's name was Leonard. I found out Leonard stayed with his girlfriend Michelle in Tulse Hill. I knew a few people who knew her and they directed me there. I approached the front door and knocked.

"Hi Michelle. Is Leonard there?"

"No," she replied, "he is out."

I said: "OK, can you call him please? As I need to speak to him today."

She promptly called him and he was there in 10 minutes. I explained the situation to him and, to my surprise, he agreed that LJ should be with him. He insisted that I brought him to the flat straight away.

I couldn't believe it – this was a man who barely bothered with his children and here he was, 9pm at night, saying that I should bring him straight away. I couldn't but wonder why he accepted this arrangement so easily. I thought it was for his own selfish reasons – to exploit the system.

I was left with no choice but to say to my six-year-old son, "OK LJ I will take you to your daddy." That same evening, at 10pm to be precise, LJ went to officially live with his dad.

Leonard and Michelle separated a few months later. Leonard was given a property in Kennington for him and LJ. They seemed happy and settled.

LJ's dad placed him in a school opposite to my home so he could pop in anytime he wanted. From what I could see, LJ's dad was doing very well bringing him up. I therefore decided to step back and allow his dad to remain in control. Seven years later, when I received that life-changing call, I was overwhelmed with feelings of shock, confusion and astonishment.

In January 2010, I decided that in October I would take a 10-day trip to Ghana, west Africa. It would have been my first holiday away in years without any children, just adults; newlywed Mr Richard and Mrs Camelia Frimpong and Shaun, Camelia's 20-year-old brother.

The six-week holiday was coming to an end and LJ had no school to start in September because he was permanently excluded – hence the £6 argument. The school had offered a place to LJ which they called a "centre" – where children go when they have no school that will accept them. I told them, "Hell no! He will not be going there, I will find him a school myself!" I soon realised it wasn't that easy.

It was now September 2010 and LJ had also been permanently excluded from the school his dad had placed him in. I had a big problem as to what I was going to do with LJ while away. LJ was on bail to appear at Balham's Juvenile Court on October 18th 2010 for theft of a pedal bike. YES A PEDAL BIKE – can you believe it? The police were really taking the mick. Anything that was happening in the local area, our home was the first place they would come to. I was fed up of it, I was fed up of the police and I was most definitely fed up with LJ. My kitchen knives were rapidly disappearing and I would find them either in the pockets of LJ's jeans or hoodies while doing his washing. It was getting exhausting.

I hadn't spoken to LJ's dad since the call I received from the police in June and he hadn't bothered to contact me either. I decided that I would call him.

"Leonard, it's me. I am going to Ghana in October and I intend to take LJ with me. This will cost £600. Can you… " before I could finish my sentence, he said "Yes?"

With 14 days before leaving for Ghana, LJ was still adamant that he was not coming with us. I had to get dark on him, as they say.

"Do you really think I want you behind me? You are only coming because no one in the family is willing to look after you, so take that suitcase and make sure, by next week, it's packed!" I firmly informed LJ. I slammed the door behind me, reached out to God and prayed: "God please help me get this boy on the plane."

The countdown began. I would routinely check the suitcase to see if LJ had put anything in it and there was nothing.

With one day to go, LJ still hadn't put anything in his suitcase. He was pissing me off by the second. Then, out of nowhere, LJ asked, "Is there a TV where we're going? Because I am packing my PlayStation."

"Thank you Lord, thank you!" I cried. "You can bring anything," I responded.

Boy, I wasn't expecting that. You see, what LJ didn't know was that this dickhead had big plans for him in Ghana as far back from when he had been permanently excluded from his first school. At that time, I had decided boarding school in Ghana would be perfect for LJ. With Richard originating from Ghana, he travelled two weeks prior to LJ and myself to set things in motion. I asked Richard to find me a school that was very basic with no luxuries.

I remember the day we left for Heathrow airport. Even Leonard came with us and hired transport for the whole family. It felt like a day trip to the seaside, as so many family members came to see us off. Unknowing to LJ, they all came to say goodbye to him.

October 17th 2010 was the day we arrived in Ghana. This is a memorable day for me. Richard had rented us a huge house with en suite rooms. It was lovely. We had our own driver, everything was perfect. Shaun and LJ loved the sun, the food and obviously the PlayStation. By now, it was day three of LJ living in a new country. LJ didn't have a clue that, in just seven days' time, he would be staying in Ghana indefinitely.

On day six, Richard arranged for LJ to visit the boarding school he would be attending. He would also sit an entrance exam and meet the principal on this day. The school was called De-youngster International School. International meant that the teaching method would be the same as in the UK. The school terms were the same as in the UK, which was handy for me due to the fact that I worked in Trinity Boys School in Shirley, Croydon.

It was now day four and I still hadn't told LJ my plan. Truth be known, I was scared to tell him I was leaving him in a strange country. Don't get me wrong, there was no doubt in my mind that LJ would be OK. He was 6'2", very handsome and softly spoken and, for some reason, this always worked in his favour. I knew he would be able to defend himself in boarding school, but he wasn't in the United Kingdom. My only concern was that they spoke more than 250 languages and dialects, although English was widely spoken throughout the country.

On day five, we decided to go to the Arts Centre. I had been given a list of items that LJ would need before he could enter the boarding house. We therefore agreed we would split into two groups, males and females, and do some shopping. Richard, Shaun, LJ and the driver went north, while Camelia and I went south. I made up my mind to inform LJ of my plan later that evening.

It was not more than an hour into our shopping trip when Camelia and I noticed a huge crowd forming. Camelia said she could see Richard amongst the crowd and, as we got closer, I could see Shaun.

The driver began walking towards us apologising over and over, "Sorry madam, sorry madam. I didn't know."

"Boarding school mum, boarding school? Are you leaving me here? You lot are really leaving me here?" I looked at LJ, looked at the driver and back at LJ.

The driver and LJ had got into a heated argument because LJ wanted to buy a knife to bring back to the United Kingdom. The driver had told LJ he would not be allowed to keep a knife in boarding school. By the time I got to the crowd, it was all over. I witnessed LJ silently crying. He looked petrified, nervous, but most of all stunned. For the first time in years, I could see a scared and very angry little boy.

We all just stood there, very afraid of what he would do next. I just remember loads of people looking at us and lots of commotion, not sure what they were saying or thinking.

"Shit," I said, "someone needs to do something."

Out of nowhere, a stranger spoke in Twi, which seemed to get rid of the crowd. I quickly asked the driver to get the car.

We went to a restaurant and, even two hours after finding out, LJ continuously bored into me. I tried to avoid any eye contact and deliberately sat away from him. However, every time I looked up, he was staring back at me.

"Shit," I said to Camelia, "he's looking at me." I kept thinking this boy is going to kill me tonight. Camelia replied, "I know, at least you tried and we still have his return ticket."

To which I replied, "Are you mad? Look at the anger in his face, do you think I am bringing him back to London? Hell no! He needs some serious discipline and I am leaving his ass right here in Ghana!"

From that day, I knew whatever I said from that moment on would determine LJ's future. That night I let him know.

"This is Africa and I can do whatever I want with you, this DICKHEAD is running things from now on, and yes, you are staying here, and yes, I will be leaving you in five days' time with your passport. Tomorrow you will sit the exam and be nice to the principal. If you try to sabotage by scoring low in the exam, they will still take you, but they will simply put you with the younger children, so you choose."

That night, Camelia stayed with me. I locked my door and pushed the wardrobe in front of it. I was so scared. In the morning, LJ's face was still the same, but he got in the car, took the exam, was polite to the principal and even smiled a few times at the boarding school students, but not at me. I was still getting the looks, but I didn't care because I knew I was in control and so did he. We were in Africa!

We had a few more days left before LJ was going into his new school and I wanted to make him feel comfortable, but nothing I did was working, he hated me. Occasionally, I thought this experience had taught him to respect his elders and maybe I should bring him back as suggested by Camelia earlier, but I knew this was just a mother's emotions speaking, so I pulled myself back on track and said my famous, "HELL NO!"

The last day came and we all escorted LJ to his school. It was early evening, so he went straight to the boarding dorms. All items that were going to the boarding house had to be laid out on a long table for the bishop to examine. Bishop was the boarding house master.

Bishop was a pleasant man, dark in complexion, tall, but a little overweight. He ticked off all the items and asked LJ, in a deep-spoken voice, "Do you want to keep your phone in the dormitory?"

LJ replied, "Yes!"

The bishop continued by saying in his deep voice, "Let me see your phone. What is your password?"

"I'm not giving you my PIN," LJ replied.

The bishop turned to me and said, "Mum, take this phone home. No PIN, no entry."

Quickly LJ blurted out, "4457."

The bishop deleted videos and other things out of his phone and then read out the rules to him. The bishop ended by saying: "My name is Bishop, please call me Bishop."

Oh! Wow, fuck, damn, I said to myself, tell him again, tell him again!

I looked at Camelia and we both smiled at Bishop. The Bishop then called a student and introduced him to LJ. "This is Jonathan, your new friend," he said. From an angry frown, a smile appeared on LJ's face.

"You cool yeah?" For me, that was a very good sign. LJ immediately had someone who he would 100% be able to relate to. Bishop continued reading a few rules and with that, it was time to say goodbye to my son.

I kissed him and I gave him the best advice that, for me, would help him in a foreign country,

"Keep your mouth shut and your eyes and ears open. You can excel, you can do this LJ, you must aim high." That was the moment when LJ's life-changing journey began.

I called Bishop very early the next morning and was told that LJ was in prayers. "Amen," I said to myself.

In life, there are things that always come back to your mind from time to time. For me, leaving LJ in Ghana actually felt like a burden lifted off my shoulders, even though I knew my journey was just starting in terms of my son. Not only was I determined to take him off the streets of London, which I did, but I also decided that there was no way my child was going to be a statistic to the British Government. I didn't bring him into this world so that the system could take him out before he had discovered and accomplished his real potential.

I returned to Ghana nine months later. Nothing could have prepared me for the changes I witnessed in my son. I was proud of him.

Who would have thought that a holiday to Ghana would have been the blind spot I needed in order to turn the future of my son around? I never thought for one minute that Ghana would become my son's home for almost three years.

Donna Caddle

Email: Destineelove7@googlemail.com

*"Those who think they know better, know nothing.
Better must come."*

Donna Serena Caddle was born on 26th February 1970, at Barking Hospital, Essex, to Caribbean parents, Veneta and Winston Caddle. She is a sister to one sibling. She attended Furze Infants, Furze Junior Schools and Warren Secondary School in Chadwell Heath, Essex and The John Loughborough Seventh Day Adventist Secondary School, Tottenham. Donna lived in Chadwell Heath from the age of 2. Raised in both the UK and in Barbados from the age of 12, where she continued with her secondary education. Donna returned to the UK at the age of 19, pursuing her further education at Redbridge Technical College and Havering College of Further Education. From there she went into employment in the private sector as a secretary within the NHS.

In 1993, at the age of 24, she became a first time mother which took over her life. She continued to work part-time and relished the love of having her first child, which was a great challenge. In 2000, she decided to leave the UK and make a home in Barbados. However, this was not to be and she returned in 2001 to start her life again. In 2004, she became a mum for the second time.

Her journey continued when her love for music enabled her to set up an instrumental music group within her church. She then decided she wanted to play music and venture into radio presenting. Her ambition was to be a news presenter. Her passion for music allowed her to work for a number of radio stations. In 2002, she began her radio presenting journey as "Lady Destinee", presenting talk and musical programmes on Blues Fm, Riddimbusta, Krystal Radio, Galaxy Radio, Destinemedia and Venture FM.

In 2013, she rebranded herself as "Empress Destinee", setting up her vision – an online radio station called Real Love Radio, which supports and features mainly UK artists. This is her second greatest achievement!

The Journey Continues

Taking the flight and thinking, why is this a 'new challenge'?

Saying farewell to the loved ones I will be leaving behind, including my son, was heart wrenching. The tears wouldn't stop flowing. Contemplating if it was the right decision, saying "yes" was not the comforting words I was longing for. Hearing a voice saying, "Come on, look forward, it will be hard, but you will be fine." Those words still resonate until this day.

Embarking on a new challenge is something we never take lightly. That small voice in my head was telling me, "OK, let go and give this 'challenge' my all. It's my life!"

There I was sitting on the plane, tearful, angry, regretful, even thinking, is it even what I want? All those questions swirling round and round. Can I ever get over this disappointment? This was the second major decision, apart from deciding to be a mother, that would be life changing.

Thoughts were drifting back to leaving the UK, arriving in the new millennium to become a wife! Wow, excitement and glee all rolled in one. Giving up, yes, giving up the material gain to start anew? Why? What is wrong with being in the country you were born in? Great Britain, with all the opportunities of moving forward with your career? Was I out of my mind? Or was I thinking of the future? Yes, again it's the future and the meaning of the word 'family'. That was why I was moving from this rock in the north of the Atlantic Ocean. Being on that beautiful island Barbados was going to be my dream come true!

Here I was, sitting on a plane again, my thoughts were not on getting back to the cold unsociable country in which I was born. I was having doubts, big doubts. How could this dream become a nightmare? Who understood my thought process? Could I answer those questions? No, it was a blame me situation – blame those who tore my life apart. Heavy were my eyes and I wanted to just jump off the plane and get my life back. Go back to my family and to those who I knew valued my friendship. I was getting more and more tired, yet I knew I had to go.

The country I lived in since the age of 12 was strange and weird. School was horrible, "Oh look, it's the English girl." I had been thrown in at the deep end and it was the start of my independence. No parents, just my brother and I staying with extended family we hardly knew and had only communicated with on the phone.

The decision was not one I'd wanted my parents to make, so there it was and off I went. Overseas, into an educational system that focused on your education with persistence and ruled with a 'rod'. From that day, my childhood changed. Was I going to live without my parents who were planning on returning, one day? Can I settle into this school and be as studious as my counterparts? I really wanted to go back home to England. Children can be cruel, but I knew I was not one of them. I could hear my mum telling me, "Do your best, don't worry about anything or anyone, just do your work." My family consisted of my mother, father and my brother. It was a pressured household with Christianity at the helm. A strict home, it was, however, in its own way filled with love. I had what I needed, not what I wanted.

The time spent in this strange country was the start of my journey through life.

I met people along the way who shaped and fashioned my life. I grew to love the country I once hated to be in. The dynamics of my immediate family was never the same since 1981. Seeing my mum again was five years down the line and, from that point onwards, it became an emotional journey. The pressures of life took a lot to readjust to and I was beginning to wonder why I was in this situation as a child. I had left all my friends and family in the UK, where I wanted so desperately to return and rekindle that union.

Here I was with my extended family and the segregation was real. I had minimal communication with my maternal grandmother, who was more into the other grandchildren and her immediate family, even though my brother and myself were in her care. The whole family was dictated to and run by the one aunt who tore my life apart. Was I to blame? It was the start of my self-doubt, my confidence was shattered and my deportment became one of seclusion. "Fend for yourself," I would say, "be helpful and show them you can 'fit' in." Could I fit in? I didn't know. "Too sensitive," was my description. "She doesn't take part with the others," they would say. It went on and on.

When the phone rang, I knew it was my mum calling to see how things were and each time I would say, "I'm OK mum," but I wasn't. Deep down I was in so much pain and wanted my parents to come and get me, just me. My brother – he was fine, he belonged. Yet I kept asking myself, so what is really wrong with me? I was not as 'great' as the Caribbeans would describe a person who thought they were 'too good' or better than others. No, I was brought up to have manners, respect and ensure my character displayed that of a staunch Christian – that was it.

With this in mind, I would write in my diary my feelings and thoughts, just to keep myself in a spirit of not being alone, but the cry was stifling. There was no privacy to be had and sharing with others was not my thing. My thing was being with my own family, not being thrown into a family I hardly knew. My granddad would go out early in the morning with his horse and cart and return at dusk. My grandmother would go into the plantation grounds, which were adjacent to our home, and toil the land until noon. We would be up with the crows and go into the yard with the animals – the black belly sheep, the chickens, the pigs and of course the outside bathroom. "My, my, my, what am I doing here again?" would come into my mind. This was the bane of my life. Going to use the bathroom and there it was, a wooden toilet with a six-foot drop – horrible, cold, damp and smelly. The existence was REAL. Boiling the hot water to wash with a bucket and taking myself back into the house. Not to mention the laundry – this was a scrubbing board and metal bath equipped with blue soap for your whites. This was me – a British girl getting used to the Caribbean life.

My paternal grandfather lived a few miles from my maternal grandparents and that was my 'escape' on a Sunday. Walking to his home and just being away was a delight. I would pack my bag for the day and go to see him along with my brother. There he would sit behind the louvres and watch as the people in the village would pass on by and shout, "Morning Caddle."

This was something you had to get used to. People greeting you in the morning, afternoon and evening or whenever they would see you, a form of respect. I was used to being on my own with no unnecessary interruptions, just me and my books and my thoughts. Going there I would meet people who treated me more like family than those whom I stayed with. They appreciated me, valued me and welcomed me into their homes as part of them. Friendships were formed and kept.

When the visit ended, it was back to the lonely life with the family I began to despise. My grandmother did all she could, but had no control really on her household. Granddad would arrive home, see to his animals, then sit in the doorway with his massive cup of drink and bowl of food until he fell asleep. The yard dog would always try to sneak a piece from the bowl. That was the fun part and those were the good days.

My thoughts drifted between my current residence and the UK – there was no comparison between the two. That life to me was the best, there I was 'me'. Here in this hot country, I was living a selfless, protective life. Nothing I had was mine, it had to be shared. With two other families in the same home, along with my brother and myself, we were full to the rafters. I had to share a bedroom with two others and I was never included in going places with the rest of the family. This was the exclusion I would face. Then there was a revelation, call it a 'reprieve from the Lord'. The betrayal was there in the form of that aunt who was meant to take care of us. Instead, she treated me as if I was not welcome.

The days went by and I would write to my mum telling her how I was feeling and being treated. These letters were given to my aunt and I would trust her to go and post them when she visited Bridgetown to sell the goods. It was then and only then, I realised in my absence, while at school, my personal belongings would be rummaged through and I knew there was no privacy. Writing my thoughts down was all that kept me sane and in touch with my parents, but it was to end. The thought of being banished and a message being sent to my parents, 'come and get your child' was a persistent chorus which rang out throughout the house. The dislike coming from the whole household grew more and more, like I was tainted.

Yet, truth be told, I had kept a secret of abuse that no one knew was happening. Two cousins and their sordid way of interfering with me, they thought was interesting. As a child, I matured in the places most girls hadn't. Once they thought I was asleep, they would touch me in places. This was not something I chose to disclose to my aunt, as it was her son. I chose not to disclose this to my mum, because it was her niece. I continued to keep it a secret until the day it stopped and I chose not to allow it to continue.

The letter was a cry for help. The time came for me to leave – I left with my brother and my uncle took us in. The love was there and I felt it back for the first time since coming to Barbados. That was the start of my journey as a young woman in a country that shaped me for the better. Was it meant to happen? Was it meant to go the way it had gone? I wondered. From then onwards, it was a journey that continued. Living with family was not ideal, but it was better than where I first started. They said I was not part of their family, they called me all kinds of names and the accusations still came and tried to taint my character. I eventually got over the initial rejection.

From rejection to learning to live again. Regaining my childhood, my teenage years were then grasped to the maximum. I started to love church again, playing in a musical group, picking up my talent that was within me. I started singing and forming valuable friendships that have lasted until today. Continuing to take life as it came, I became responsible for my own actions. The word 'trust' was a major buzz word for me.

The poignant happiness that resonated from going to a school I eventually settled into, with friends I could be myself around and a boyfriend – yes, I had admirers. I had this one male friend who was persistent, even though he broke my heart in years to come, he existed and was real to me and I was real to him. He never gave up talking with me and keeping me alive with his care and attention. It was all platonic and I looked forward to seeing him, especially going to church when he was there.

Then one friend within our circle became ill – one minute she was there, the next, she was gone. We had shared good times – who we would marry, how many children we would have and what our homes would be like. That day was the worst day I could imagine. Aged 15 years old and she was gone – my dearest friend and confidante, gone. Those tears were the first to express the loss of life, which was part of reality. Why does it hurt when we lose someone? She was not supposed to leave, she was meant to become of age, like we all would. That part of my journey was again a direction that threw me. Recovery took years and, even then, she would revisit my journey in life with her name coming into conversation, just like she was, vibrant and full of excitement. That light was one that kept coming through.

My life became a whirlwind of events. My mum arrived in Barbados to finally take over and be with her children. My dad remained to keep the other home functioning and to maintain his family back in the UK. The dynamics changed again, and the journey took another turn.

I sat there going through what 'could have been' what 'I should have done', and this kept me from seeing through the clouds that were overshadowing my despair. That journey up in the clouds landed and I couldn't remember a thing, it was a long flight in the sky and I cried myself to sleep.

My home, my refuge, my new destination was here. I resided with friends and family and I could no longer hold onto that dream of being a dutiful wife and a consistent parent. Where was my 'destiny' and where would it take me? I encapsulated all of my dreams and told myself: "This too will come to pass." It became reality – having to accept the past was not going to be part of my future. To make my future was totally in my control.

I loved my time just for that short moment of relishing in being a beautiful bride adorned for her groom, having the attention and the long-awaited ceremony was no longer surreal. It happened. Sharing the dream, sharing the moment for that split second, it came to an abrupt halt. Feelings of anger, forgiveness, spirituality and Christianity took precedence – just to express the feelings that were coming into play. Can you deal with the man you loved for over 13 years actually doing this to you? Are you accepting his faults, are you yourself perfect? Questions and answers on a postcard was what I wanted to scream and shout at strangers, just for clarification. The purpose and intensity of my mere existence became a big shift in my destiny. This was going to take me to the next level.

Why do you think you are not worthy? Are you not a talented, intelligent, loving woman? After the storm will be the calm. My beautiful second mother would be there to hand. Every moment of her life until 2008, she shaped me with her knowledge and understanding. Was it even possible for me to have a better life back on the rock in Great Britain? "Yes, it will be rough, but you will be fine," she said. I shaped my existence. God is love and love is God. I started to breathe again. The crying was still there, but there was never any denial as the clouds started to part and the sun began to shine.

The storm was indeed passing. The thought of giving up never left my mind. How can I have allowed for these events to take hold of my life? The fight was REAL, the anguish was REAL and my whole existence continued to be REAL.

My heartbeat was my son, whom I'd left behind. It was not the perfect situation. Was history going to repeat itself? Of course, in some way or form, it did and my parents did their best to keep him going with his education and keep him from missing his mum. My determination to help him succeed in his childhood was by staying focused. Work, work, work. You have to have a purpose. The time was coming nearer and nearer, when the sun was starting to shine more. The places I had to live I never thought I would have to be in. The times I would long to be on my own and live by myself, I had to keep holding onto that thought. What kept me from falling? The love of my family. My destiny – the journey continues...

Jacqueline Francis

www.jacqueline-francis.com
Email: info@jacqueline-francis.com
Facebook: jacquelinebfrancis
Twitter: @jackyfrancis
Instagram: @jacquelinefrancis17

*'If you forgive those that sin against you, your heavenly
Father will forgive you. But if you refuse to forgive others,
your Father will not forgive your sins.'*
Matthew 6: 14-15

Jacqueline Francis is a teacher, businesswoman, mentor and writer of poems. She graduated from the University of Westminster in 2003. In 2005, she graduated from the University of Greenwich attaining her Postgraduate Certificate in Education (PGCE).

Jacqueline has over 10 years' experience as a teacher. Her enthusiasm took her to Canada in 2011, where she herself studied and taught English to foreign students.

On her return to the UK in 2012, she set about restructuring the business she started 14 years ago and still continues to manage today.

In 2015, she rekindled her passion for reading books and tried her hand at writing poetry. In late 2015, she successfully had one of her poems published in an anthology called, Contrasting Visions.

Jacqueline's story sets about illustrating what transpired when she became:

- Ostracised and estranged from her siblings;
- The rifts that can derive from duplicitous behaviour of siblings;
- The impact that it had on the rest of the family; and
- Overcoming estrangement and ostracism.

She also underlines the emotional turmoil such as anger, sadness and grief of being rejected. Her story is unique because it highlights sibling envy and jealousy that did not originate from her childhood, nor from the competitiveness of parents, as some people often suggest.

Jacqueline hopes that by putting pen to paper, she can create a platform to inspire others to have an open conversation about ostracism and estrangement, and how dealing with envy and jealousy can easily be overcome.

Jacqueline grew up in Harlesden, in north-west London, and now resides with her family in Ealing.

Green Eyes

"Quick! Hurry up! Your Mum's coming!" shouted Heather as she bolted around the corner. Barbara looked up to see Heather running down the road, her knees knocking together ready to buckle under her. Barbara looked up from her game of hopscotch, one foot hopping like a uniped. She eyed Heather confusingly until she remembered that she'd sent her to act as a look out, to let her know when her mum was coming. She shouldn't have been on the street, but she detested the confines of playing within the gate.

Waving her hands in the air, Heather said, "Get in the gate, quick she's coming!" Heather was now standing in front of Barbara with both hands on her side, breathless, panting as if she had just competed in the 100 metres race. She flicked one of her long plaits out of her eyes. "Your Mum's coming!" she breathed heavily.

It was not unusual for her mother to allow Barbara and her sisters to play out with the other children on the street, as long as they promised to play within the gate boundaries.

"I told you not to go outside the gate; you're going to get caught one of these days, it's not worth the risk of a beating!" exclaimed Lauren.

"Course it is. I won't get caught, so I won't get a beating, will I?" joked Barbara, sticking her tongue out. Mum walked up to the gate, saddled with two heavy shopping bags, four plantains poked out from one of the bags and a bunch of green bananas from the other.

"Everything alright?" Mum asked.

Two small voices chirped, "Yes Mum."

"Come and help me with the bags."

Lauren was Barbara's younger sister, who was six years younger than her older sister Claudette. They lived in a three-bedroom flat in north-west London. Their mother, a nurse, worked the night shifts. Their father was a painter and decorator. Barbara and Lauren shared a bedroom in their first floor flat at 51a Drayton Road, Harlesden. The large bunk bed took up most of the space, which only left room for a single wardrobe and dresser. Her sister Claudette occupied the smallest room at the front of the house, dominated by the single bed against the wall. The room seemed bigger, because the door opened outward allowing for a chest of drawers, a small wardrobe and a chair under the window.

Barbara hated being in the flat, she felt boxed in. She enjoyed the buzz and vibrancy of the streets. Children from numbers 43, 51 and 70 were always about - even Tracy, the little white girl from number 55 with her perfectly manicured blond ponytail, white knee-high socks and pressed clothes. The pulsating street created energy when the children were out. When she was denied her freedom, Barbara would climb up on the piano in the front room, pulling the net curtains back so she could get a better view, occasionally joined by her sister Lauren. When Claudette wasn't home, Barbara would sneak into her bedroom, kneel on the chair and slide open the single sash window, pushing her body out as far as she could to see all the way down the road.

"Are you coming out today? We need you and Lauren to make up the numbers for rounders," called Deanna, their neighbour from number 51.

"I can't, Mum won't let me!" Barbara shouted back.

Deanna was joined by the boys from number 43 and two of the kids from number 70, who were yelling at the tops of their voices. Engrossed in the activities below, Barbara was startled when she felt a tug on the waistband of her blue pleated skirt. It was Claudette.

"Get out my room!" shouted Claudette. Barbara hadn't even noticed that her sister had come home.

"How many times do I have to tell you? Don't come in my room!" Claudette barked angrily. "Stay in your own room. I'm sick of you lot coming in here."

"Alright, alright, keep your hair on," retorted Barbara as she pushed past.

Claudette was two years older than Barbara. Her speech was articulate. She was learning to play the piano, schooled by the choirmaster who lived at number 7. All three sisters attended choir practice on Friday evenings. There was always a reluctance to attend practice because the church was always cold, dark and musty, smelling of stale incense. She would feel the cold seeping through the layers of clothes she wore. Her teeth chattered as she mouthed the hymns the other choristers were singing, "Holy, holy, holy, Lord God Almighty."

Barbara felt a jab in her side, "Come on sing! The sooner we do this, the sooner we can go home," whispered Claudette.

"Barbara! Dad's ready, we're waiting in the car!" Claudette shouted from the bottom of the stairs. It was their regular weekend visit to their aunt's house at Winchelsea Road, where she always had 'blues' parties. On arrival, the children were ushered into the front room, leaving the adults to enjoy the music. There were uncles and aunts, friends and work colleagues from the Heinz factory in Harlesden. Every week they gathered to drink, smoke, play dominoes and listening to the likes of "Cherry Oh Baby" or "My Boy Lollipop", a selection of reggae music by Bob Marley or Gregory Isaacs, to name a few. It was tiresome.

Starting secondary school excited Barbara. Claudette had already been attending John Kelly Girls School in Neasden. Now they would go together. In a few years, Lauren would follow. Evenings were spent debating what house and groups Barbara would be in, based on academic ability.

"They might put me in Dollis, same as you!" Barbara exclaimed.

"I don't think so. I'm in Alpha of course, the highest group. I don't think you'll be though, maybe in group Three."

Barbara gave Claudette the side eye and said sarcastically, "Of course you are."

Barbara had made friends easily, joining the school netball team, awarded the role of vice captain or captain on several occasions. There was no incentive to be in the limelight when she was with her friends; they were always hanging around waiting for the boys in the shopping centre. She was happy to watch from afar. Boys were the last thing on Barbara's mind, she was a tomboy. What boy would be interested in her anyway?

"Barbs look, that boy over there, he wants to talk to you," whispered Janet. They were at Kingfishers youth centre. She looked over to where Janet was pointing to a good-looking boy, tall, of mixed heritage with tightly knit curly hair, staring back at her. He was the colour of Nestlé condensed milk. His name was Richmond.

"What do you think?" Janet asked.

"Yeah, he's alright."

"You play pool don't you? Go and ask him for a game. You always go after what you want anyway. So go get him, girl."

Weeks later, they were an item. When she brought him home, her sisters were astonished at how good looking he was. Barbara knew what her sisters were thinking; he was too good looking for her. What did he see in her?

At 17, she completed her first year in sixth form, but she wanted to attend college. Claudette had decided to stay on at school to complete a two-year secretarial course.

"What are you going to admin for?" asked Mum. "You could do a secretarial course, like Claudette."

"I'm not interested in typing and squiggles on pages. I've had enough of school," sighed Barbara.

"It's not squiggles, it's shorthand," Claudette commented.

"Whatever, I'm not interested." Barbara spent weeks trying to convince her Mum why it was a good idea. Her mother finally agreed.

By the time Barbara was 18, the family moved to a three-bedroom flat in Holland Road, NW10. Even though the rooms were bigger, Barbara still shared with Lauren, who was a quiet girl. Claudette had started hanging out with her older cousin and developed a social life. Barbara's social time was spent at Roundwood youth club, with her friend Yasmin from 20 Drayton Road. It was there she met the guy who would become the father of her child. By the time Barbara was 21, she had given birth to her son.

"We've bought the flat in north Wembley. Contracts were exchanged today!" Barbara shouted, running in and out of the rooms like an excited child.

"What's all the noise about?" Lauren asked.

"Where's Mum? Mum! We've exchanged contracts! We've bought the flat!"

"Praise the Lord, thank you Jesus," Mum said, clasping her hands together.

"Yeah man, that's good," Dad nodded his head.

"Does that mean I can have my own room now? When will you be moving out?" interrupted Lauren, standing in the hallway with her multi-coloured headscarf tied tightly on her head.

"Did you hear what I said? Where's Claudette? Isn't it great news?"

"You need to make sure the mortgage is paid on time then, otherwise they'll repossess the property," Claudette said, poking her head around the bathroom door.

"Do you ever have anything good to say?" Barbara flung her hands up in the air and walked off, slamming the bedroom door behind her.

Three weeks later, Barbara moved out of the family home. Her sisters never visited. By the third year, she'd grown apathetic. It wasn't the life she expected. She remembered a comment her work colleague had said: "Barbara, you're so lucky. You've got your own place. I wish I had my own flat."

Yes, she was lucky, but she wasn't happy. Her life was looking after her son, whom she loved dearly, and keeping house, while her partner spent time football training, playing matches or spending time with friends. Was this it for the next five or ten years? If so, she wanted out.

Barbara had had enough and moved back to her Mum's house. Her decision did not come lightly. Claudette took pleasure in knowing Barbara had gone back home. There was a sense of satisfaction that her younger sister had failed.

"My Mum's having a birthday party, you should come," said Carla, a work colleague. "You need cheering up."

"I'm not sure," hesitated Barbara.

"Monni and Di are coming, you can get a lift from them."

"I'll think about it."

By Monday morning, Carla was at Barbara's desk grinning.

"Barbs, did you have a good time? You know there's a guy that fancies you, he wants you to call him," Carla waved a piece of paper with a mobile number on it.

"It's not the guy that you were talking to at the party though. This one's better looking, trust me; he wants to take you out. Call him," Carla urged.

About three years into the relationship, Barbara had a daughter with that guy. When she first brought him home, again both sisters were impressed with how gorgeous he was. She could tell they admired his good looks, intelligence and confidence.

"Why don't we buy a place together?" said Barbara as they sat in a Chinese restaurant in Denmark Hill.

"We should wait a couple more years. Anyway, I want to get my new car, the Mercedes Benz I was talking to you about," he replied as he delved into his Sichuan king prawns with bamboo shoots, blathering on about what colour he should get. She watched as he emptied the remainder of the chicken noodles onto his plate.

When their seven-year relationship ended, Barbara always made sure that her children kept in contact with their dads. But she still needed to buy her own place. A year later, they were living in a three-bedroom, two-reception house.

"You've got loads of space here," said Lauren, as she roamed through the rooms with Claudette.

"Why don't you two get a mortgage? The bank won't say no. Claudette, you earn more than both of us and you've both been in your jobs for ages."

"Yes, I'll consider it," answered Claudette.

"Leo's having a party, you coming?" Lauren asked.

Leo, one of their older cousins, had been hosting parties at his house for years, just like his Mum did.

"I won't be around, I'm in south," answered Barbara, knowing that she wouldn't be missing anything. It would be reggae all night, which Barbara had had a lifetime of already.

"As always," Lauren whispered, with a look of dissatisfaction towards Claudette.

When Barbara's relationship ended, she enrolled in an evening class to study French. She had always wanted to be bilingual, plus she loved the challenge. After completing that course, she enrolled on an access course, where she met Amanda who wanted to study law at university.

"What do you want to study at uni?" inquired Amanda.

"Umm, I'm not sure. I hadn't even thought about it really."

"Everyone here is planning on going to uni. Speak to Sir."

One evening, the family were in the front room. "Guess what," Barbara said.

"What?" Claudette and Lauren replied simultaneously.

"I'm going to uni. I've been accepted at the University of Westminster to study Business Studies."

"But you work full-time, how are you gonna do that?" asked Claudette.

"You can't afford to do that, when you have a mortgage" her mother said, with an anxious look.

"Isn't uni suppose to be full-time?" questioned Lauren.

"Full-time can mean three days a week."

"Are you sure about that?" interrupted Lauren.

"Of course I'm sure!" exclaimed Barbara.

Three years later, Barbara graduated with a BA Honours Degree.

"What now for you?" questioned Jessi.

"I'm not sure. I know my son now wants to go to uni. He said I inspired him, but we need to move, there's too much trouble living around here."

Barbara and Jessi were good friends. They were like ackee and saltfish – you didn't see one without the other.

"I'll go house hunting with you if you like," Jessi said as she walked out of the house towards her car. "I'll meet you tomorrow, about ten."

"OK."

Four weeks and several viewings later, Barbara found a three-bedroom house in Ealing with a large garden. This was the one.

"Your house is so far," Lauren complained.

"It's about an extra 10 minutes' drive. By the way Lauren, what school choices are you making for your daughter? I'm definitely going to choose Marylebone, it's one of the top public schools in Westminster."

"Me too! Convent and Hearts are on the cards as well."

"Make sure you plan for the entrance tests."

"Good idea," agreed Lauren.

A year later, it came as no surprise to Barbara that her daughter had been accepted into Marylebone. The personal tutoring had paid off.

"Guess what? She got in!" Barbara said excitedly over the phone.

"That's not fair!" replied Lauren angrily.

"What do you mean? It's the only school that has accepted her. Your daughter has been accepted at two schools. What's not fair?"

"She didn't go to her interview did she? So she shouldn't have been accepted." With that, Barbara hung up the phone.

"Jessi, people keep asking me why I wasn't at Leo's party on Saturday. Macy messaged me asking why. What am I meant to say?"

"Why didn't you go?"

"No one told me about it."

"Why are you worrying about it?"

"Because this isn't the first time," Barbara said in frustration. "Macy's always asking me why I'm not at my own family parties."

"Maybe they forgot. Anyway you should be happy, we're graduating today," smiled Jessi.

They were sitting opposite each other on a Southeastern train, heading to Greenwich University, munching on KitKat and crisps, engaging in idle chit chat. She had achieved her PGCE and was now a qualified teacher. Barbara knew

Claudette wanted to go to university. She had talked about it, but she never did.

General conversations between friends raised concerns.

"Maybe they're jealous."

"That's ridiculous. They're my sisters."

"You've heard about green eyes, haven't you?"

Selective communication was the only thing that Barbara was now privy to, so in many ways, her decision to move to Canada was easy. She'd been planning this for five years. "You're so brave," everyone said. She knew that her sisters would have discussed her leaving, but their only response was to smile pleasingly. Not once did Claudette or Lauren call to see how she was settling in. Unfortunately, that same year their mother passed. Arrangements were made to book flights to Jamaica for the funeral.

"I hope you've brought something appropriate to wear," announced Claudette.

"What do you mean?"

"I know you like to wear your clothes short, so I'm just saying I hope your dress is appropriate for a funeral." Barbara felt like a child being reprimanded. She was used to the little digs, Claudette had been doing it for years. The heat in the bedroom was oppressive; the fan stood whizzing warm air.

"Look, I love fashion. So I think I know what's appropriate," retorted Barbara, walking off.

Back in the UK, Barbara and her siblings arranged to meet to tie up their mother's affairs. Lauren invited everyone to meet at her house. When Claudette arrived, there was no small talk, the sisters got straight into it. She became aware that Claudette hadn't uttered a word to her. What was her problem? She'd noticed that, when documents were handed to Claudette, she would hand them to Lauren, then Lauren would pass it to Barbara. Why would she do that? Surely she knew that Barbara would want to see the documents too? Was this a game? She'd overlooked it the first time, but Claudette did it again. When the meeting concluded, Barbara walked over to the window, looking out. She turned, facing her sisters, they both remained seated.

"Before I go, can I ask, just out of interest, do you guys have a problem with me? Is there something going on here that I don't know about?" The room was silent, only the sound of the oven fan could be heard from the kitchen.

"Look, we all know that things haven't been right for a number of years now, but you guys have ostracised me and I want to know why." She stood staring at them both, waiting for an answer.

"You think that you're better than us, don't you?" Blam! An imaginary smack in Barbara's face.

"The way you talk to people, the tone that you use!" Lauren said accusingly.

"What are you talking about?" Barbara looked confused. "I don't understand," she shifted from one foot to the other, feeling a little disconcerted. What was going on here?

"You talk to people as if you're better than them."

Barbara stood, open-mouthed. She wanted to laugh out loud, but she could only raise an unnerving smile. WOW! Did she hear that right? Her eyebrows knitted together. After a moment, taking a deep breath, she stepped forward.

"So you're telling me you both think that I've been ostracised for years, because of the way that I speak to people?" her voice sounded irritated, her left hand pulled at her bottom lip.

"And what's more, you never seem to attend any family events. We stopped… "

Barbara interrupted and gave a wry look. She couldn't believe what she was hearing.

"I know what you're referring to. You're talking about Phillip aren't you? That day when he came to the house when we lived at Holland Road?"

"Yes I am actually. It was the tone that you used when speaking to him, it wasn't right," replied Lauren.

Barbara half laughed. "Are you serious?" Not for one moment did she think that a conversation she had nearly 20 years ago with a friend would cause so much misery and resentment. Phillip hadn't been offended, so why was she?

Barbara had first met Phillip when she was about 16 years old. She'd been riding Reid's bike. He usually rode down from Dollis Hill. Phillip had walked his girlfriend Yasmin home – Yasmin had introduced them. But years later, when Phillip worked for a ladies' fashion company, he knew Barbara loved fashion so he would bring the latest garments to her. If she wasn't there, Lauren would play hostess, engaging in small talk. He was a shy, quiet, reserved person, a bit like Lauren. On one occasion when Philip visited the house, Barbara and Lauren had stood at the top of the stairs.

"Come in then, don't just stand there. Don't be an idiot, come in off the street!" Barbara shouted down.

"Don't talk to him like that Barbara, you're so rude," Lauren spoke in Phillip's defence.

"Oh shut up Lauren, it's Phillip, he knows I'm only joking." Lauren walked off as Phillip made his way up the stairs.

Barbara was dumbfounded as she drove home. Her palms were sweating as she clung onto the steering wheel. Never in a million years did she see that coming. It was all so incredulous. She replayed the conversation in her head, picking up on the fact that Claudette hadn't commented as ever, always watching from the sidelines. But then, that incident with Phillip didn't have anything to do with her. So what were her reasons?

About two years later, Lauren turned up on Barbara's doorstep unexpectedly.

"Why are you here?"

"You're not responding to my messages."

"What do you want to talk about?"

"YOU!"

Why was she really here? Both of them, with their green eyes, were angry that Barbara had snubbed them.

Those former years were lonely for Barbara, having lost her mum and not being able to talk to her family about her death. She always remembered her mother saying, before she immigrated back to Jamaica, "There's only the three of you girls here. Make sure you look after each other."

There were days when she would find herself sitting at the edge of her bed, staring out the bedroom window, just as she had as a child. This was her safe place, her legs pulled up under her chin, head resting on her knees with arms wrapped tightly around them. She didn't know whether her emotions were related to the loss of their mother or her siblings, or both. There was no one to talk to about how she felt. She tried to hold back her tears. Here she was, estranged. On days when it became too much, she would break down sobbing. If the children were in the house, she'd run to the bathroom, turning on the shower to mask the sound of her cries.

One Christmas, Lauren sent her a message requesting that they all meet and talk.

"We can either go for counselling or mediation."

Her cousin Brenda agreed to mediate. Barbara sat and listened to Lauren talk about the same BS; her trip to Canada and being in south London was added to the mix.

Brenda was shocked this had been going on for so long.

"To be honest, it makes no sense. You know you need to speak to Claudette though?"

"Yes, I will."

Claudette's text message read:

"I concur with what Lauren said at that session. This ongoing issue was raised and discussed a couple of years ago. The conclusion from the recent mediation I can gather is that there has been a lack of communication on your part and it has affected us all. I don't think I can add anything new."

She later backtracked and agreed to meet without mediation. What would have changed from the comment she had made in her text? Barbara didn't need Claudette to appease her. Even Marvin Gaye knew what was going on.

"I think we should each write a letter saying how we all felt about this issue and what we can do moving forward," commented Barbara. "What do you think?"

Dear Claudette & Lauren,

I hope this letter finds you both well. I know we haven't had the best of years, so I'm glad we took the decision to start building bridges. But I have so many questions to ask.

Where did it all go wrong? There was no sibling rivalry, so where did this resentment towards me come from? Did it ever occur to you how your treatment towards me made me feel? Or didn't you care? Was it a decision you made individually or together? I was blindsided. I didn't think my own sisters could be jealous or envious of me for living my life.

Remember when we were children, when we thought we were that trio singing group, Brown Sugar? We performed in front of the mirror singing 'Our Reggae Music', ironically the first line was, "we three are sisters of love". Or when we'd pretended to be the Three Degrees with our synchronised dancing? LOL.

I was the rebellious one as a child and a teenager, willing to take chances, hoping not to get caught. Do you recall when I was about 14 or 15, I sneaked out the house to go to a birthday party? Only I forgot my key and had to ring the bell. It must have been about 2 o'clock in the morning. Daddy answered the door, I ran past him, up the stairs into the bedroom. The next minute, Mummy comes in raising hell threatening to 'dash' water on me and call social services, cos she'd had enough. I told her 'go on then', she kissed her teeth and walk out. I started laughing. Next minute, the door flung open, and Mummy came in with a pot of cold water and threw it in my face. Lauren, you were under the covers, laughing hysterically.

Anyway.

Before we start building those bridges, I wanted to let you know that I know that this was never about the 'tone of my voice' or 'not attending family events'. This was about the limitations you placed on yourselves. This was about the choices that you both failed to make. This was about your insecurities that you wanted to lay at my door. You both sat back and wished for things, but never made them happen - with that said, I make no apologies for the choices I made for me and my children and the choices I will continue to make.

I am so glad that our children did not get caught up in this and still remain close cousins.

But you know what, I hold no malice towards you for the last 20 years. If you take anything from my letter, my message to you is to start living your life. We are all limitless in what we can achieve. Write on those blank pages and keep them turning until you've written your book.

Be happy.

Barbara

Janet Blair

Email: www.thejanetblair.com/contact/
Facebook: jpscapitaltrading
Twitter: @jpsforextrading

"Your life changes the moment you make a new, congruent, and committed decision."
Tony Robbins

Janet is an award-winning author, an extremely successful Forex Trader and an international speaker. She has more than 10 years' trading experience and now runs a thriving Forex training business. Janet has trained, coached and mentored over 1,000 people worldwide and provides her clients with simple tools to trade successfully.

Her book, *The Trading Floor*, outlines strategies and concepts to guide beginners and advanced traders to understand the Forex market.

Janet has a no-nonsense approach to her work ethic and uses past experiences to teach clients how to avoid the pitfalls of trading in the markets.

As a committed mother of two children, Janet has enjoyed the flexibility of being there and spending more time with them. Her business allows her to travel to different parts of the world, while being able to trade no matter the location.

Janet is a self-motivated, passionate and consistent trader who delivers the same attributes to her clients. Clients can expect to learn how to trade the markets effectively, which includes Forex, commodities, indices, stocks and equities.

Janet's strategies will enable clients to execute high-probability trades and build unlimited income. The training and mentoring are carefully structured to meet individual trading objectives and are designed to transform trading psychological behaviour to accelerate trading skills.

"Live the life you deserve."

Beyond True Love

One sunny afternoon, walking down the road in my local community, I saw a friend that I knew from church. Growing up in Jamaica, we were taught not to share too much about our personal lives. I took the character from my mother, who didn't 'talk much', therefore didn't speak to people. People would often say, "That girl thinks she is too nice or better than everyone."

When I arrived in the UK, I started my career in the NHS as a receptionist. I learned that people here shared their feelings. It used to upset me, as they were very inquisitive and constantly wanted to know what my plans were for the upcoming weekend. I didn't realise it was a part of the culture. Coming from Jamaica, you were taught not to share your business with others. Therefore, whenever I was asked questions about my weekend, I would answer with very few words. They would ask, "How was your weekend?" and I would reply with a simple "OK" or "fine", to shut down the conversation.

I became very close friends with a man I met in my local community. We attended the same church and he would give me a lift home after. He would watch me on a regular basis, staring at me whenever we had an event. He was very caring. As I was working in the NHS at the time, I told my girlfriend about him, who was also from Jamaica. She was in the same predicament as me, as her husband-to-be was very caring and loving. Unknowing of how the British culture worked, they would be so friendly and tell you everything.

I thought this was very warm. You felt safe around people knowing you could trust them. As a little girl, I didn't have my father around. He left our home when I was four years old, so I didn't know what it was like to be wanted and to have a man who was caring. You might say, I was looking for love, which indeed I was, living alone with my mother, who was a very quiet person.

I had a boyfriend at the age of 16. We were seeing each other for over two years and when that relationship ended, I was very sad about it. He told me that he wouldn't be able to look after me, because I was more educated than him. After all, having a British boyfriend was the cool thing!

Meeting my British boyfriend, who was also a man of God, was very good for me. It was very fulfilling to have someone you loved and who was very caring. Every woman desires to get married at some stage, especially if you grew up in the church.

Christianity

I became a Christian at the age of 12. I had my mind set on finding someone in the church – someone who loved God and wanted to carry out his work, including being a husband who loved his wife unconditionally.

My boyfriend proposed to me, and I was over the moon knowing that I would soon I'd be married. Growing up in the church, as a 'church girl' you are told you have about six months to get married. Looking back on it, how can you know someone in six months and get married? We were so in love, we decided to get married. However, to my surprise, other people saw signs he was no good for me, but I was blinded by love and made excuses for his actions. I didn't want to acknowledge there was a problem. Growing up without a father meant I didn't understand the behaviour of a man.

Lost in Love

I was unable to tell the difference between a man who cared and loved me, and a man who was also insecure and got angry at the smallest things. He wanted his way most of the time and didn't get on with his siblings or father. These were all signs that the relationship wouldn't work.

He asked me to marry him, and I said yes, as every woman growing up in church dreams of getting married in a bid to prevent being 'left on the shelf'. It saddens me that pastors all over the world, in particular from the Caribbean background, don't explain the pros and cons of marriage. You are taught that you must get married quickly, just in case you SIN, not taking into account the future of the couple and having to live together.

On 1st September 1990, when we got married. We had a fantastic wedding with 300 guests, including church members and family. It was a joyful and happy day – I felt on top of the world. The next day, we went off on our honeymoon to Tenerife, which was fabulous as well. We were able to travel to different countries every year.

As the man of the house, he would always take care of the bills, as he believed the man should provide for the home. We opened a joint account and were told by other couples it was best to have our salary going into one account. I didn't know that my husband was very particular about spending. Having these traits wasn't bad, however, there needed to be a balance. After opening the joint account, I had to buy things for the house, including groceriers and paying the bills. He would complain about me spending money on food that he would enjoy on a weekly basis. Especially household items – he would ask why we needed them. I continued to maintain our relationship, as we had a great marriage.

I gradually realised that having a joint account was not working for us, as it was causing a lot of friction and conflict. I would go shopping for shoes or clothes and would not tell him what I bought. I would hide new clothing or shoes in the closet and wait for an opportunity to wear them. He would often ask, "What did you buy?" and I would lie and tell him that I got it at a discounted price in the sales. I wouldn't dare give away the real price tag. I kept this going for years.

As the years went by, I decided to have a separate account for my salary, as I didn't want to be asked every week what I had bought. I was very conservative in my spending and only spent when I needed to. I would buy things for the house and bring them out gradually, especially when we had visitors. He would smile, as our visitors complimented us on how lovely the decorations, fixtures and fittings in the house looked. Knowing he didn't pay for any of the items, it made me cringe when our guests would compliment him.

I would advise you to have a joint and a separate account when you get married, as money can be one of the main destroyers in a marriage.

Signs Started Displaying Themselves

It was almost two years into the marriage when I became pregnant. Until this day, I can remember my ex throwing my clothes outside the doorway and telling me to leave our matrimonial home. Being pregnant at the time, I really can't remember what I did for him to get so angry and upset. I didn't have to do anything for him to be angry. He would come home from work and tell me that the house looked like a 'pig sty', as he expected me to clean up daily but we both had full-time jobs.

I would come home from work and get straight in the kitchen, while he came home and complained about the state of the house. He would change his clothes and just relax. I thought it was so unfair for him to moan about the house, as it was tidy. Remember, we were both a working couple – the only time for a good overall clean would be at the weekend.

When he came home, he would expect a cup of tea, which I didn't mind, to be given to him. If the tea was not to his liking, he would complain and wanted another one made. As I would be in the kitchen when he got home, I had to stop what I was doing to make him a cup of tea, which I didn't mind doing if I was not tied up doing other things. I enjoyed cooking, therefore I would ensure he had the best Caribbean dishes cooked.

One evening, I remember placing his dinner on the table. He delayed coming to the table to eat his dinner and when he finally came, he got angry that the food was too cold and insisted I warmed it up. We both sat at the dinner table expecting to have dinner together. He expected me to leave my dinner and warm up his food, while mine turned cold. I would do it all the time, but one day I decided not to fall for his spoilt, childish attitude and told him to go and warm it up himself. "Who told you to say that?" he shouted at me. I was so frightened, I started to cry, as I did all I could to make this man happy. The way he treated me during the years of our marriage were all bottled up.

Bottled-Up Emotions

Being in a relationship where I kept quiet to avoid conflict was not healthy. It can be very bad for your health and emotional well-being.

Over the years, things started to reveal themselves more and more. I was living with a man who claimed to be born in church, living a Godly life. His prayer would move mountains. He was a great gospel singer. Growing up in the Caribbean as a Christian, you are taught to behave Christ-like. Your lifestyle should be one that is blameless, not living in anger or fear. You should live a life with joy and fulfilment as you are a child of God and, by your fruits, people would know you are a Christian.

Mental Abuse

I didn't realise that I was going through abuse with my ex. I always thought that someone throwing physical punches was not acceptable. Having mental torture on a weekly basis is not good for someone to live a life of fulfilment either. Both physical and mental abuse are equally damaging.

One of my friends would always look at me during my marriage and say, "That woman don't look happy." I would try at all times to keep the relationship going, the happiness in our marriage going, as I believed no one needed to know what was going on in our home. I would pray to God on a daily basis that things would change. I kept quiet and kept bottling things up inside. People would often see us outside together and say, "What a happy couple," as he was very affectionate and loving outside of the matrimonial home.

I wasn't able to drive. Therefore, my ex would drive me everywhere I wanted to go if I was not able to take public transport. One day, my family invited us for dinner. He was upset with me and didn't take me to my family event. He told me to make my own way. I was pregnant at the time. I started to cry inside again; I informed my family that I wouldn't be coming as they lived 20 miles away from us. From that day, I made my mind up that I was going to learn how to drive and purchased my car. I was very determined, failed my test about three times as I was so nervous. So nervous that, on one of my tests, my legs started to shake to the point you could hear it on the pedals. On the fourth time, I passed. I was over the moon that I could drive. I wouldn't need to ask him to take me anywhere. It gave me a feeling of independence. Obviously, he never liked it, as he wanted to be in total control of my life.

Take Control of Your Destiny

From this day forward, I started to take control of my destiny. I decided I will never have anyone tell me how I should live, what I can do and where I can go.

I attended an event held by the motivational speaker Tony Robbins. I had travelled from London to Australia to attend Date with Destiny 2016. One of the sessions was looking back at your past and how people had treated you in life. Tony mentioned, if you can speak with that person, then these are the words you should say: "I thank you. Please forgive. I love you."

When I heard Tony mention these words, I started to reflect on my life and look at the person I was. A very strong and courageous woman who was determined, no matter what life had to offer. I vowed to always make something good out of a bad situation. Being able to forgive my now ex-husband gave me such a relief and healing. One of the greatest healing tools in life is being able to forgive and move on. The Bible always teaches us to forgive, as Christ has forgiven us.

"Forgiveness is not an occasional act; it is a constant attitude."
Martin Luther King, Jr.

Putting life into perspective, I decided to get myself an education in order to get a well-paid job. Again, I came across another hurdle. After having my first daughter, I decided to become a medical secretary. I started to work as a receptionist in the NHS, but felt this wasn't what God had planned for my life. My husband didn't like the fact that I was working on my education. He wanted me to be a 'stay at home mum'. For you to move to the next level, you have to continue growing by educating yourself.

I signed up to become a medical secretary by pursuing a secretarial course in this field. I would always be looking out for opportunities at work where I could move up the career ladder, in addition to looking after my family financially. And one day, as I was looking through the weekly job opportunities, I saw a medical secretary position. I applied and was called for an interview. I was successful and stayed within this field for a few years, as I was looking after my daughter. I would take my daughter with me on my journey to work and drop her off at the nursery before work, then collect her after. It was a blessing to have a nursery on site.

After a couple of years, I decided my purpose on this earth was not just to be a medical secretary or supervisor, surely there are other careers I can use my skills and knowledge in. I decided to study for an MBA. This again didn't go down well with my husband, as we now had our second child, our son. I got accepted into Brunel University after being turned down by another. I went to my boss and asked if I could take every Monday off to attend uni. Thank God I was offered a day release.

During my studies, I found it very difficult, as I had to be a mother and a wife while studying at the same time. I didn't receive any help or support from him. He told me that it was a piece of paper, it would never take me anywhere and I wouldn't achieve anything from having it. He mentioned that there are so many people out there who have degrees and master's and don't even have a job. Hearing these words hurt. I wanted to quit because of the discouragement. I was made to feel guilty for studying and being a wife and mother.

The tongue is like a two-edged sword. I certainly wasn't going to allow these words to affect me. I brushed myself off the next day – I was even more determined to finish my studies. I continued for the next two years, completed my studies and graduated with an MBA. I was so delighted to receive such a high qualification, as none of my family had ever achieved a degree or master's. It gave me great joy just to know that I could complete this qualification.

Deep down, I know he didn't appreciate that I'd managed to get a qualification that he didn't pursue, although he attended my graduation.

After being in church for most of my life, I didn't realise that, just because people called themselves Christians, it didn't mean they didn't have hidden agendas. Have you heard about the 'dark side'? I never thought this was possible. Being saved at age 12, I believed that, once you have given your life to the Lord, it should be that you are a completely changed person.

Having lived with my husband for 16 years, I decided enough was enough. I could not live this life anymore. In fact, the previous year, I informed him that, "I will not be tolerating his behaviour in our relationship and the year 2006 needs to be different."

Life Begins at 40
I turned 40 years old in 2006 and life had to change. However, he thought I was joking and never took me seriously. When we first met, I was a very shy person and wouldn't stand up for myself. I finally got the courage to face the facts, as I didn't want to bring my children up in this environment, for them to think it's normal for a husband and wife to live in this manner.

In that same year, I learned how to trade the Forex markets, as I wanted financial freedom. I'm so glad I continued along this journey, as I now teach and trade using simple strategies, which you can use too (www.thejanetblair.com).

In June 2006, I took my children and went to my mum's one-bedroom flat just to find a peaceful life. We somehow made things work living in a one-bedroom flat. Obviously, that didn't go down well with him. He called my friends, family and the police to try to restore the marriage. Never again would I be fooled by just face value or be blinded by love!

Lara Alao

www.larafamosa.com
Email: info@larafamosa.com
Facebook: Lara Famosa
Twitter: @LaraFamosa

*"Surround Yourself Only With People Who
Are Going to Take You Higher."*
Oprah Winfrey

Lara is a successful entrepreneur, author and mentor. She is a diligent professional who has a great passion for empowering women and helping them embrace their true potential and worth. Pursuing her passion for motivating and inspiring others, she went on to found 'Gravity Angels', a series of conferences and seminars for female empowerment, and 'Embrace U', an innovative self-esteem programme for girls. Lara is passionate about building dynamic and engaged environments that will improve the lives of communities. She believes this starts from motivating and inspiring women of all ages in finding purpose in both their personal and professional lives.

Lara is particularly skilled at educating women about the tricks and trades of succeeding in the competitive entrepreneurial world of today and has guided many into having a more outstanding and remarkable life.

She is a resilient professional who holds an exceptional sense of creativity. Her confident personality assists her in striving for excellence in her professional career.

Lara believes her goal in life is simple – to raise happy, confident, healthy and determined young adults. Lara also has a degree in architecture and is naturally very creative. One of her many dreams is to one day own her own boutique hotel. Lara enjoys cooking and greatly cherishes spending time with her family and friends.

Accepting One Of Life's Many Paths

I thought everything was perfect. I had a pretty happy family and a good life.

I just did not see it coming. I hit the most horrific bump in the road – then it felt like I was on a fast-moving train headed for a cliff, and I couldn't jump off. It was like I was watching a movie and couldn't believe I was part of it.

In 2007, I lost my son unexpectedly without any warning.

He was due on 4th January 2007. I remember getting up in the morning, going to the bathroom and the contractions starting. I called my mother to come over to stay with my two girls. When she arrived, my husband and I rushed to the hospital.

I got to the hospital very much in pain from the contractions accompanied, with a ton of excitement that I was about to give birth. I had not taken any medication, just gas and air, as I'd already had two kids, so I just expected the same process. Go into hospital, have the baby and go home. But nothing prepared me for what was coming.

The midwife came and asked me to lay on the bed so she could monitor the baby. I lay there, praying for her to hurry before the next contraction came. She put the straps on and I just kept doing my breathing techniques, as I had done with all the births. I looked up and there was a weird look on her face. She looked down at me, and her face went completely red.

She said, "I'm sorry Lara... there's no heartbeat."

I looked up at her, "Pardon?" It's not like I didn't hear her the first time, but I wasn't sure I wanted to hear her say it again. She repeated herself while stroking my arm.

"What do you mean there's no heartbeat?" I said. It just didn't register. "I mean, no, seriously, what do you mean there's no heartbeat?" I continued on, I was so desperate. "But I can feel the contractions. I can feel him." I just waited. I didn't know what to think or how to feel.

I was still having the contractions. This time, I was numb to the pain, as my brain and emotions went haywire and the realisation of what the nurse had just told me was beginning to sink in. I don't know what went through my head at that point. I just remember going numb and completely overwhelmed by this emotional roller coaster. I was in shock.

She left the room, at which point I looked up at my husband and whispered the word, "Sorry." That was about all I could say at that point. I was sorry for everything. Was I being punished for something? What did I do wrong?

The nurse returned to tell me that I was going to have to give birth to the baby naturally. I was going to have to give birth and go through the contractions, knowing full well that the baby would not breathe when he came out.

The emotions are coming back now as I write this. They are just all so raw. I had to have an epidural. I was so motionless, I didn't care any more. They could do anything they wanted. I was screaming inside my head, but the words were not coming out of my mouth, "WHY?" I'd given birth to two girls without any hassle. I had two daughters at home. They were both natural births, I didn't have to go through this.

I had the epidural and, after a few hours, I gave birth. He was a perfect baby boy and there was absolutely nothing out of place except he had no breath.

They put him in a cot at the other end of the room and I just remember staring over. The nurse asked if I wanted to carry him and I just shook my head from side to side. I knew at that moment, if I carried him, I would have that connection and that would kill me even more. To this day, I have regretted not carrying him, just for that one moment. There are so many moments in life that I wish I could take back and change. That one moment is a major regret for me. I just looked at him and thought, how will I get through this?

Shortly after the birth, the doctor came to check on me. Then there was another doctor and, before I knew it, there were many doctors rallying around me. All I remembered was seeing a lot of blood.

I was taken to another room with medical equipment all around. I saw them looking down at me and doing stuff below. I was still numb and I could hardly speak.

My husband was outside in scrubs standing at the doorway. Next thing, they shut the door, but he tried to peep through the gaps of the curtains. Then, they pulled them shut so he could not see anything. I looked up to the ceiling, "WHY ME? What's going on?" I was now screaming in my head.

I woke up and I had tubes coming out of my arms. They had made an insertion in my neck. I had a hole in my neck, with a tube going down my throat and wires coming out of my arms. "What the hell is going on? What happened? I only came to give birth to my son," I groaned painfully. The emotional pain was more intense. I always squirm at the sight of needles and now to see all this? I felt numb to it all. I had no idea how long I had been there for or what day it was.

I looked around the room, but there was nobody who looked familiar. I went into shock again. Everything seemed so surreal. There were about five other people in the huge ward, all with different apparatus or machines around them

– both men and women. Is this really happening to me? I thought for the umpteenth time.

A few moments later, a nurse came over. At that point, I still couldn't believe I was in such a critical state. As she started talking, I remembered she was the kind nurse who had taken care of me in the maternity unit. She explained what had happened to me. I could see her lips moving, but nothing was entering my ears. I looked over at the door – ITU (intensive care unit). HUH?

The nurse asked if I was aware of what had happened to me. She felt very sorry and came to pay her condolences. They were really grateful that I was still alive, because it was touch and go at some points. They had to give me a blood transfusion, because I was losing so much blood and they couldn't find a way for to stop it.

I was still completely dazed and confused. Throughout the pregnancy, there was just nothing out of place. The baby was sound; there were no hiccups in between. She was just as confused as I was, as to why I'd lost him.

As she spoke, amidst my grief, a thought hit me and I needed to be sure there was still hope. "Nurse, please tell me the truth, do I still have my womb?"

She looked at me with that red face again like, oh my God. Then she said, "I really don't know."

Oh my God, I screamed in my mind. I thought they had removed my womb. I won't have any more children. What am I going to do? They should have known. The tears started streaming down again.

"Please calm down," she said, "I'm going to go and find out. I will be back to tell you, okay? " She left immediately, but it felt like I was waiting for eternity. She eventually came back, looked at me and smiled. I interpreted that smile as a positive response. "Lara, there is no cause for alarm, you still have your womb." I breathed a sigh of relief.

At that point, I thought, well, I'm going to try again. He's going to come back. He will come back to me. I didn't care if that thought line was just me being superstitious, or maybe reincarnation happens in movies alone. I just wanted my boy back, if not now, in my next pregnancy.

I remember looking up at the ceiling, thinking why me? What did I do wrong? Where have I done? Did I say something to somebody? Did I offend someone? I believed very much in energy, people's negative energy around me and people not wishing me well.

There were so many questions I wanted to ask. There was so much I wanted to understand that I just didn't. Nobody could explain it to me. The pain was heart-wrenching. I couldn't be comforted due to the sorrow that engulfed me.

Later that day, my husband came to visit me in the hospital. He had been so great during this period. He was supportive, trying to make me comfortable, even though he was grieving too. He also had looked forward to having a son, but now that hope had been squashed in the cold grip of death.

We were both happy when we knew it was a son, since we already have two beautiful daughters. Everything was just going fine until this unfortunate event.

There was a moment in that ITU that I looked over at the lady in front of me. She was an Indian lady. All her family came in and greeted her. I thought she had gone through something similar to me.

In a sense, I felt comfort knowing that it wasn't just me in this pain and other people had such experiences. But that didn't make me change my mind about the fact that I felt the Lord had betrayed and abandoned me.

When I saw that woman, at least I had somebody to talk to. I felt close to her, some sort of connection with her. Then somebody came through the door with a baby - it was a baby boy. My heart sank and I couldn't even pretend to be happy for her.

She had gone through something similar to me, but her baby was alive. I felt alone again – she had her baby and I didn't. I remember when her family came in, they had red powder on their foreheads, – they were Hindu.

I felt cheated, I prayed a lot, and I did everything right, yet I didn't have my baby. To make the situation worse, I was in intensive care with tubes coming out - left, right, and centre of me. I'm sure this woman prayed as well. She was just human like me, and she still had her baby. That was something that has always been at the back of my mind.

I have always wondered what I was to learn from this situation, as I have always believed that whenever things do not go my way, there is something for me to learn. I examine myself to know what actions contributed to whatever the issue is at that point in time. I try to always look from the outside into any situation and where I had fault. I HAD DONE NOTHING WRONG, SO WHAT IS THE LESSON HERE? Many unanswered questions went through my mind, and I doubted if I would ever have an answer.

God made the female body in an amazing way to prepare it for childbearing. I had to pump milk for weeks following the birth and death of my son. Some days I would cry for hours on end. My arms ached as if I had dead weight. I would put my arm in such a way, and it was almost like there was a weight on my stomach, like I used to feel during the pregnancy, but there was nothing there.

I started questioning God, "Why did you put me through all of this? You prepared my mind and body, and yet you took this boy away - why? What did I do?"

When I was in the hospital, my family came around to visit me. They made me feel so happy and took my mind away from things by talking and joking with me. I let myself feel comforted and hoped for the best.

They were good to me, making me grateful for the gift of family. When they left that day, I remembered a midwife coming to check my blood pressure and realising it was very high. She said she wanted to move me to another room because of this.

She put me in what I would call a broom cupboard. It was so cold. My husband had to go home and bring a blanket to the hospital for me so I could sleep. He stayed with me the whole night. I knew he was cold, but he wouldn't leave my side. He insisted on staying with me. No one came to check on me the whole evening. All night, I could hear babies crying down the corridor. The nurse had put me back in the maternity ward where mothers had just had their babies. I couldn't bring myself to even say anything or complain. I said to my husband, "I just want to go home please."

This was an experience I would not have wished on any of my worst enemies. That was a horrible experience and so uncaring of the nurse to make me stay with other mothers, knowing what I just went through. I went home, and I questioned a lot. I had to go back into mother mode. My sister and mother had been looking after the home while I was in the hospital. When I got home, it was like I was seeing it again for the first time. My husband had taken away the cot and they had put things away. I decided to keep a few of the things I bought for him. I still have them till this day. My mother and sister had to get back to their lives, so I took up my responsibility as a mother to my daughters again.

After doing the school run, I would come home and cry most days. Then get up, pick the girls up from school, do the housework, get dinner ready then lock myself in the room to cry. This became a regular routine.

Women are amazing creatures. It's amazing how much we go through, but we never show the outside world. I just didn't want the girls to see me crying all the time.

We had to go back a few weeks later to go and speak to the consultant. The consultant said, "You have two beautiful daughters. You had a major operation. You had blood transfusions. You know, we saved your life? Don't try again; just leave it at that. You have your children. Don't try anymore. Just be happy with what you have."

I wasn't happy, I just wanted more. There's nothing wrong with wanting more, is there? Growing up, I always wanted four children. That's what I wanted, to have my four children and be happy. When the consultant said, "Don't have any more kids," in my mind I started preparing myself to say, "This is it. Thank you for my daughters."

As time went on, I still wanted to understand exactly what had happened and why it had happened. I had to go back again for another consultation. This time, it was with a different consultant. She seemed more compassionate towards what I had been through. I had to ask the question again. "Can I have more children? Because I've been told I can't, and I don't understand why."

She said without a second thought, "Yes, of course. Why not?" She continued, "Just get your body back in shape, and then you can try again. We will monitor you closely." In my head, that was confirmation. I'm going to have my boy back. He's coming back to me.

It's funny how, as women, we hide so much when we're in pain. Even though we are pained, we still smile. When we're going through stuff, we still smile. That's how I remember it. I remember, after coming out of the hospital and seeing my girls, my heart melted for them, because they too were ready and prepared for a little brother.

I know it affected my eldest in many ways. When I got home, my mother and sister were there. They had dinner ready. They had been keeping the house for me, making sure the girls were okay, looking after them, cooking dinner daily, talking to my husband and so on.

Although I was in this state of mourning and pain, I still had to go on. I had to go on for the children I had, the children who were waiting for me, the children who were still calling me mother.

As women, we don't allow circumstances to bring us down. We just go on and on, and we smile through it all. Those blind spots will come, and they will hit you like a brick in the back of your head. They will just come from nowhere and yet we still rise, we still show up. We still put that lipstick on like before and dress up, and we still smile.

There was a period of time, while at home in the mornings, I would watch the 'Oprah Winfrey Show'. I was into Oprah Winfrey so much. She helped get me through that period. I'm so thankful for her. All my friends and family know that about me. Whenever I got the opportunity in those days, I would bring up a teaching from Oprah. My friends would roll their eyes and say, "Here she goes again about Oprah." I used to talk and watch Oprah religiously every day when I got home from the school run. She got me through a lot. I listened to her, and it was around that time *The Secret* and *The Law of Attraction* books were popular. I started to question, "I did not attract what happened to me, did I?"

Oprah started a series with Erkhart Tolle, who taught 'The Power of Now' and being in a place of constant gratitude. I had to learn to surrender to what had happened, stop the questioning and just become comfortable of not knowing 'Why me?' Sometimes, the act of letting go of things is an act greater than defending or hanging on.

I have come to cope with this. What I tell myself is 'life is for learning'. But some things happen that I just have to accept, good or bad. If I do not learn from it, someone else may get something from it. I always think of that Indian woman and how she still had her son. She was Hindu. I now know not to judge anyone.

I've seen so many people go through things. There is nothing special about what I went through or who I am in this world. We all have a story to tell. We all go through things, but it's how we deal with those things that determine our future and the future of those around us. We are just here to live the life we have been given to our full potential, no matter what religion or background we are from. Whatever cards you are dealt, deal with them and move on.

At what point did I see this coming? I didn't see it coming at all. I realised there's so much in this life that could be changed. There's so much we can do that you don't need to be stagnant and wait. There is always a better tomorrow.

Martina Barnett

Email: Martina@InsideOut.com
Facebook: Inside Out UK
Twitter: InsideOutuk

*"That which does not kill us, makes us stronger,
live life to the fullest and focus on the positive."*

Martina is by far one of the most talented actresses, singer/ songwriters of her time.

In 2000, Martina studied A-Level Performing Arts at Croydon College. She also studied Operatic Vocal Training and performed many classical pieces.

She made her first appearance as a teenager on 'Wish Baby', a feature film directed by Simon Sprackling, and made several other appearances in various feature films, that eventually helped her secure her first leading role as 'Diva' in a play called 'Big Voices', directed by Dawn Walton at the Royal Shakespeare Company. Martina then went on to perform as a gospel singer in a play directed by Glenn Supple called 'Vexed' at the Royal Court Theatre.

Martina's artistic achievements have taken her to stages such as the Theatre Royal Stratford, Bernie Grants Art

Centre, Jermyn Street Theatre, Bloomsbury Theatre, Albany Theatre, Hackney Empire, Roundhouse and Wembley Arena, to mention a few.

Since then, Martina has been working with an international, intercultural artistic organisation called 'Roots & Routes', which entails travelling around Europe collaborating on artistic productions creating new music, dance and media with European artists. The work is then performed at different festivals across Europe. Among the midst of this, Martina made an appearance on the first interactive TV series 'Dubplate Drama'.

Her determination and drive ensures she is constantly working, whether on personal development, growing her business and entrepreneurial achievements or creating new projects. Along with an easy-going nature and down-to-earth character, Martina is also an intelligent and delightful person.

Martina has completed a number of courses including:

- BA Honours degree in Applied Performing Arts
- Urban Voice courses: Gateway to music and reality check
- National diploma in Music and Theatre
- Foundation degree in Performing Arts

Martina believes you should release your glow within - by just being you; using your talents, skills and experiences to express yourself. Vibrate from love and think positively - enjoying every moment life has to offer.

Diamond Under Pressure

This chapter in my life made me realise who was around me. I started to really see people for who they truly were. This is when I started to see and find myself. Who has got your back? You have got your back – the quicker you know this, the better. I'm thankful for my struggle, because without it, I wouldn't have stumbled across my strength. Remember, everyone has a different heart and mind, so whatever you would do for someone and how you treat them, you can't necessarily expect the same in return.

I was about to start a tour in Europe. I had finished university and was ready to embark on my career. I had been fortunate enough to be in prestigious places, around high-profile people, networking and learning new skills. Since leaving school, I had studied and had a vision that I had been working towards. My life was not just about me, as I have a son to guide and protect. I have to set an example for him, as his first role model – this was to do the right things in life and work hard.

At that point in my life, I would help my mum a lot, as she had not been well and also had young children to care for. My life was working, studying and being around my family. I was all about having a big dream and focusing on achieving it. And although very ambitious and focused, I still believe we need a balance. Having friends, socialising and letting your hair down occasionally is necessary.

Summer, August 2008, I was at my mum's house in bed. It was early evening, but I had my cousin's granddad's funeral to attend the next day. I was contemplating going home that evening or just go home in the morning to get my clothes. I then got a call from my best friend. It was her friend's birthday. A thought came to me – maybe I should chill as I have somewhere to go in the morning. I ignored it. It was summertime and you want to go out and enjoy the bubbly sweet air and memories it brings. My best friend at the time did not have a car but you know how you do, you roll out.

We went out to Brixton to celebrate. We were in a club dancing, having fun and just enjoying ourselves. I had one brandy and Coke. When we left there, I dropped my best friend off and then planned to drop her friend home after. On route, I looked both ways to pull out onto another road, then, BANG!

A car had hit into the driver's side of my car! I was in shock and felt angry, as I was actually in a courtesy car. For fuck's sake! I thought to myself. It was only a week and a half ago that I had just managed to walk away with my life from another car crash I was in.

My own car was written off and now the courtesy car was fucked. How am I going to get home now? How am I going to get my son to school? For a night out that I could have passed on... really?!

I got out of the car to ask the man, "What happened? Had he not seen me? And if not, why not? Why was he driving at such a speed?" A fire engine and ambulance had arrived at the scene. When the police arrived, I was sitting in the ambulance. They asked me to come out of the ambulance to do a breath test, which I did.

In this moment, I was standing talking to the police and I had a feeling inside me that I just wanted to run and keep on running. I thought it would just make things worse, so I stood up to deal with the situation I was in. At the time I was not aware that the police could have done a blood test to see if I had alcohol in my system. I had three attempts at the test. They told me that, if I did not successfully complete the test on the third try, I would be arrested and have to complete a breath test at the police station. I don't know why I failed, as I did everything they said.

Still they said I did not blow hard enough on all three attempts, therefore I was arrested. I was arrested in what they call 'front stack', which is when you are considered 'not a threat'. This means that the cuffs are put on with your arms in front of you. If you are considered a threat, you are arrested with your hands behind your back. I only know this now, due to my experience.

The police were young, but there was an older lady officer with them. The main officers dealing with me were a man and woman, who seemed eager on the job and had an air of arrogance about them. The police car was parked on the right corner of the opposite road to where we were standing. The police officer pulled the handcuffs, which dug into my wrists. I advised the officer that she was hurting me, but she did nothing. I started to get angry and told her that I was not a dog, therefore she did not need to pull me. By the time I could get the sentence out of my mouth, I had two officers pick me up by my elbows and the other pull me by my cuffed wrists to the left corner of the opposite street to where we were standing, so we were now aligned to where the police car was parked. To this day, I do not understand why they did not bring me straight to the car.

The male officer then proceeded to crush my ribs into the railings, with which I told him that he was hurting me and crushing my ribs and that I could not breathe. At this point, the officer did not know if I was pregnant or had any internal injuries from the car crash. The girl who I was with called my best friend to tell her what had happened. As she was not far away, she came. I told her to call my mum to let her know what was happening.

The officers then proceeded to put me on the floor, face down, still cuffed. I had a male officer sitting on my back and the female officer holding my legs. The officers then called for back up. From what I remember, four police vans were called and two police cars with dogs. When I was on the floor, I looked at my hands and started to think about two people I knew who were killed in police custody. I remembered Brian Douglas, who was my husband's uncle. It was a high-profile case which, to this day, the family have not received justice for. The other person was Horace Walker, who was my nephew's grandfather. As they ran through my mind while I was on the floor, I decided in that moment they were not going to kill me. I found this source of inner strength that I was not being killed tonight – not by them.

It took them a while to get me into the van. I thought if they can do this to me in front of people, what are they going to do to me the van? It took about 10 officers. They dragged, pulled and pushed me, all while I was still cuffed. I even had a chunk of hair pulled out.

Eventually they got me into the police van. I was laid out on the van floor. I had two male officers laying on me, one across my ribs and another across my legs. The police woman then proceeded to grab me by the throat, digging her nails into my windpipe while I laid handcuffed with two grown men laying over my body.

When I got to the police station, they carried me like a piece of meat, ready to be cooked on a spit roast. My legs were strapped together and my hands still cuffed. Then they were holding me in the air, trying to ask me questions. I refused to answer. I told them I needed medical attention.

They then handcuffed my arms behind my back and left me on the floor. My mum and sister arrived at the police station to find out what was going on. I said that I was not telling them my name until I received medical attention. They finally let me see the station doctor. When I was talking to the doctor, the female officer left the door ajar and was listening to me telling the doctor what had happened.

I said to the doctor that I would not speak to her with the officer standing at the door, as I did not see the reason for her to be listening. Is that even legal? The doctor asked the officer to shut the door. The doctor was not helpful – I guess she would not be, as they all work together. The same police woman then took my fingerprints and I asked her why she did what she did, I was so angry at this point. I was no longer cuffed and I was in the room with her alone. I wanted to knock her the fuck out and tear her to pieces. I had to think that I was now locked in the police station and if I did this, there would be no telling what they would do to me. I had to control the anger and rage I was feeling.

I was then held for 12 hours in a cell battered – a vulnerable female, mother, daughter, sister, niece, aunty. In pain, thinking over what really had happened, how did I end up here after a so-called 'fun night out' and after being in a car crash? Crazy. That thought then came back to me, and in that moment I thought to myself, why did I not listen to it? I did the breath test at the station, which showed I was under the limit. To my amazement, I was then interviewed about assaulting the two officers, one male and one female. Nothing about the car crash or the man involved in the accident was ever mentioned. I was then charged with assaulting two police officers. I was released, battered and bruised, on bail.

On leaving the station, my mum came to pick me up and was glad I was still alive. I went to the hospital to get my injuries recorded, then home to have a bath to soothe my body. The next day I went to another hospital as my friend's sister was working in the photograph department. I asked her to take some photos of my injuries, which I am grateful to her for doing. I was taken to court, where the car crash was never mentioned, and charged with assaulting two PCs. I appealed the case, which is classed as a new case, meaning whatever the judge decided before was disregarded. In the appeal, I was given the same community service and fine that was given in the first case. With the appeal, they would not give me a jury – I wonder why?

The night I had the crash was my 'blind spot'. I never dreamt for one minute that having a car crash would lead to me being arrested, beaten and being treated like an animal. I didn't see that coming. I have heard and seen on TV how racist and vile the police can be, but up to that point, I had never experienced it. I always thought they were here to help individuals, not beat and traumatise them for no apparent reason. This is how you can see that they abuse their position and take advantage of the law that they are supposed to uphold. It is easy to go by hearsay but when you see and feel for yourself what they are capable of, it's a different story. I cannot judge every officer by my experience, as you have to treat people how they treat you.

I had no previous convictions or any other since my unjust experience. It was a hard time for me. Through it all, it has made me stronger, more determined to reach my goals and helped me to become more aware of myself and others. Most of all, I am still alive, which I can only be grateful for.

Since my credituliby had been tarnished, I set up my own organisation as it became hard for me to get jobs due to now having a criminal record for being assaulted and nearly killed.

If I had committed the crime, then fair enough, I would have to put my hands up and face the consequences. I used to work for the police doing drama and dance workshops for the summer programmes for young people. This just made me see how destructive society is.

For people who have committed a crime and have done their time for making a mistake in their life or did whatever they had to do for survival, who is anybody else in society to judge them? This is preventing them from moving forward in their lives, having a massive effect on some people. They can get into very deep depression, which can spiral into a host of things, such as drinking or taking drugs. Their cycle continues back to crimes of self-destruction. If I was not a fighter in this life, where would I be now? I did go through depression, frustration and lots of questioning. Why did this happen to me? What's going on in my life? Which led me back to myself. I then went on my journey of self-development. Who am I? What is my purpose? Who are my friends? What do people who call themselves friends want from me? Are they my friend? What is a friend? Time for change.

When you go on the journey of self-development, you start to look at your mindset. What are you attracting into your life? What vibration is your frequency? Was this my wake up call? There have been many times I would go to an interview and have to explain what had happened. At interviews, usually you have your CRB (now known as a DBS) done, which highlights the so-called crime committed in black and white. The amount of times I have relived the pain of telling the story just to get a job to help my family move forward and to progress in my life; talking while trying to hold back tears – then I would not end up getting the job. So long after the bruises heal and the pain from the body fade, the wound is constantly reopened by society.

Diamond under pressure. I am definitely a diamond. The most powerful thing that has come out of this experience is the LOVE of self, knowing of self, listening to self and being reconnected to self. Every person, situation and object you interact with is to help you learn about you. Life's journey to me is evolution and growth of spirit through the flesh. I am excited about living/unfolding my greatness and royalty, which is my birthright.

Ruby Antoine-Poleon

www.acalmbirth.com
Email: info@acalmbirth.com

"Giving birth should be your greatest achievement,
not your greatest fear."
Jane Weideman

Ruby is a hypnobirthing practitioner and mother, practising since 2014. She gave birth to her son using hypnobirthing techniques and was so fulfilled by the process that it inspired her to gain a greater understanding of the methods used. So she trained to become a qualified practitioner.

She first discovered hypnobirthing many years before she actually fell pregnant, and instantly recognised the positive benefits that such a birth can create.

When the time came to give birth to her own baby, she naturally chose the hypnobirthing option. It provided a considerably reduced labour period and delivery and, more importantly, provided her with the ability and inner strength to tap into the body's own natural methods of dealing with pain relief. She didn't want any medication during childbirth, she wanted the birth to be as natural as possible.

Hypnobirthing provided this solution and it supported her in controlling pain without the need for prescribed drugs or medication of any description.

She opted for the popular and original Mongan Method. She felt totally empowered by the Mongan Method, a programme that enabled her to tap into her inner strength and understanding, greater self-awareness and a belief in self. By maintaining her focus and remaining calm, she was able to achieve the birth scenario she wanted. To her ultimate surprise, the method also aroused a deeper connection between her and her unborn baby – a bond and connection that exists to this day.

Hypnobirthing defies what popular culture tells us childbirth is all about. It inspires a knowledge that fear has no place in the delivery room, and instead of fearing the pain of giving birth, Ruby learned to embrace it. She looked forward to meeting her new baby and welcoming him into the world. Thanks to the level of control she was able to create, her son's birth was stress and pain free. It genuinely was an enjoyable experience.

Through education and empowerment, Ruby possesses a genuine passion to share this knowledge, and pass it on to other expectant mums. Ruby is truly passionate about it and wants to explain the process and introduce other mothers to be to the ultimate satisfaction hypnobirthing can bring to childbirth.

Ruby's teaching style is informal, relaxed and light. Participants in her classes enjoy the course and always find time to laugh together. She welcomes question time and discussion sessions from which everyone can learn.

Ruby practises throughout London and Kent in the privacy of her clients' or her own home. Ruby lives in Kent.

The Journey

I started my job because it was something that I always wanted to do. I love travelling, exploring different cultures, learning new things and just discovering a different way of life. But I knew I wanted more, so I gave myself a time frame and a few expectations.

I soon found out that, unless I was willing to play the game, it wasn't going to be achieved. They didn't get my personality, my character and we were from completely different worlds.

A world that meant if I got drunk with you and hung around with you in my free time, I would progress. A world that meant if I kept my head down and did a fantastic job, I got sidelined for someone who was more vocal in expressing the work which they had done. I decided I would be more sociable, but I wouldn't suppress my personality any longer because it's who I am.

Life is about progression and elevation and, while every other area of my life was moving forward, my work life remained stagnant. I tried but it just didn't work, so I accepted it. I loved my job, the opportunities and lifestyle it availed, so I stayed. I wanted more, but that old saying 'timing is everything' rang true. I still needed to do something more, I was always thinking.

Although I worked full-time, I did part-time hours, which meant I had a lot of days off. So I asked myself, what could

I do on my days off? Could I start something that I could bring to work and do in my free time while at work? What was I interested in? What excited me?

I discovered there was an opportunity to diversify my working role and the company would make exceptions in my working commitment to permit me to undergo the necessary training. But I procrastinated and missed the boat! So, determined to continue this path of becoming a beauty therapist, I researched accredited open courses.

Although I had a lot of days off in comparison to someone who works a regular full-time job, knowing which days I had free proved to be a little tricky because, like most things, you need to know what you're doing in advance. I had the class schedule months in advance, but I could only confirm my attendance six weeks in advance at the most, as that was the earliest I received my roster publication. So, needless to say, it didn't always work out.

Furthermore, it would take me longer to finish the course than the students with whom I started the class as a result of this, but that didn't phase me. I was prepared to work around my roster and, thankfully, the school was accommodating.

And oh… did I mention I was planning a wedding?

I got married, became pregnant and to me it was the perfect opportunity to complete my studies and get all of my practical work completed. I would now be home more often, so it would be easier and quicker to achieve. Going forward, I would become properly part-time. I'd always wanted to be part-time but the only way I could achieve this, it would seem, was if I were to be sick or pregnant.

I carried my coursework to the office with me and my workbook took pride of place on my desk. When it was quiet, I would read and take notes. Friends and family allowed me to practise on them and even took days off work to be my model for my exams.

It was at this time, while I was at work on my placement, that the reality of giving birth began to dawn on me. The further I got into my pregnancy, the fears that a lot of women have about birthing started to surface.

I was stuck in an environment where most people viewed giving birth negatively. Nobody had positive stories to tell and the medicalisation of childbirth was glamourised. I didn't know what the alternative was, but I knew I didn't want that, despite me being scared at the same time.

I wanted a natural birth, however, I was petrified of having one. Nevertheless, I had decided I owed it to myself to at least try it for my first child and, if it was too unbearable, I would consider another method for my subsequent births.

My mother had previously gone on a course where she learnt to walk on hot coals and bent a metal pole with her neck! So I asked her if she thought there was something similar for childbirth? She said probably, and off she went, researching away. She sent me a link to something called hypnobirthing. I skimmed it and thought, nah that's NOT for me, that's some airy, fairy, nonsensical matter, and I'm just not interested.

A few weeks went by, I went to the salon for some treatment and was offered some magazines. I declined the offer as I knew I wouldn't read them. However, the therapist still brought me a selection. I respectfully flicked through them. I opened the first and started flicking away looking at the pictures, then I came to an article about hypnobirthing!

This time, I decided I'd give it some attention.

I read the article and realised it was something I had heard an actress talk about on a TV breakfast show some years ago, when pregnancy for me was such a distant idea. But I had only caught the tail end of her story, which I liked, however, I had conveniently missed the part where she had used the terminology 'hypnobirthing'.

I took notes on my phone and sought out a practitioner local to me. I didn't realise there were so many options, but the most in-depth package was the one offered by someone who taught the Mongan Method. The Mongan Method was devised by Marie Mongan, who just happened to be the person who created hypnobirthing.

I contacted the practitioner to make necessary enquiries, discussed it with my husband and enrolled on the course. My husband was completely shocked that I'd even consider something like that, as it was totally new to me. I was willing to do ANYTHING I could, if it meant I could have a PAIN FREE birth NATURALLY!

We attended the first session and I was expecting to see all kinds of paraphernalia, but I didn't. The only thing I saw that could remotely be considered as paraphernalia, were some crystals – I still wasn't convinced. I asked my mum to come and sit in on the next session to be doubly sure that no hocus pocus was going on. She said, "Don't be so silly," but still came along and, of course, there was nothing untoward going on.

I found the classes very informative. I had no expectations really, as I didn't really know what hypnobirthing was about, nor did I know how in-depth the classes were. I was doing the NHS antenatal classes, as well as the NCT ones, so this really prepared me for it and where both classes encouraged drugs and bed births. Hypnobirthing was the polar opposite!

Most hypnobirthing mums opt for water births at home, totally unmedicated! This was a very new concept for me.

You were taught the pros and cons of having a hospital birth, the benefits of having a natural birth, the effects of drugs on both yourself and your baby, and how to question and enquire rather than accept what is being told.

Often, because we see a person dressed in uniform, we take it for granted they have our best intentions at heart.

When sometimes, it's simply a case of best practice or following procedure for them, which may not be what's best or right for you.

The course was informative and thought provoking.

I am by no means a hippie or tree hugger, but if you knew me before, you'd never imagine I would parent the way in which I do, be as calm as I am, or simply put, be so 'alternative' yet so 'normal', if that makes any sense at all?

I was pregnant on a journey and hypnobirthing came at the right time. It changed my perspective on pregnancy; it taught me the importance of a father's role throughout pregnancy and especially during labour; helped me to bond with my baby in utero; allowed me to consider my baby more and generally shaped me into the person I am today.

I can truly say I am a better person and mother for it, and I love that. I have a special bond with my son and I wouldn't want it any other way.

I enjoyed the course, my pregnancy and birth. I had an amazing water birth, and birthed my son in 25 minutes. I didn't even realise I was in labour, so much so that I trained to become a hypnobirthing practitioner - 'A Calm Birth' was born!

I think every pregnant woman and every expectant father deserves to have the birthing outcome which THEY desire. Too many times parents' wishes are overridden and, because we don't know any better, we just accept it as the norm. Bhen actually, you have a voice, and that voice is very powerful and has a right to be heard.

I love the knowledge and empowerment that the course promotes, and it's not in a forceful way either. Rather, it's about you knowing the options available to you and making the decision that's best for you and your baby – there's no 'one size fits all'. What works for some may not necessarily work for others, so it's about being open and exploring different avenues.

I'm a passionate advocate of birthing in a calm manner, getting in touch with your body and your baby, because I see the benefits to all involved. I've lived, witnessed and taught it. It's an awesome experience, and to know that you have all of the tools within you to ensure you have an amazingly calm AND natural birthing experience is awe-inspiring. It's self-motivating and liberating.

A calm birth is for everyone, no matter if it's your first or second birth, if you're planning a home birth or a hospital birth, a natural birth or planned caesarean – it doesn't matter which course your birth takes, a calm birth will help.

Every mother deserves to experience this at least once and every baby born is entitled to this rite of passage.

Tanganyika

www.marineqweenz.com
Instagram: @_JaynGreen
Periscope: @_JaynGreen

"Right temporarily defeated is stronger than evil triumphant."
Martin Luther King Jr.

Tanganyika is an advocate and consultant in the cannabis industry. She is the CEO of cannabis brand Jayn Green, which offers all-natural skincare products to the masses.

Tanganyika is an author, videographer and more, but her most important title is United States Marine Corps Veteran. Tanganyika uses cannabis to combat the symptoms of PTSD, stress and physical ailments suffered while in combat. She is the co-founder of Marine Qweenz, a non-profit organisation which aims to improve, educate, empower and inspire other veterans to overcome the residuals of serving.

Tanganyika is an Art Institute of Washington graduate and a phenomenal public speaker. She has previously worked with Black Enterprise, NAACP and Women Grow. She currently resides in Pasadena, California.

The Power In Green Flowers

"Let me hit that," I heard myself say to him.

I remembered it so vividly, like it happened yesterday. We were standing on top of a high ass bunker somewhere in the middle of northern Iraq. I was looking out, staring towards the horizon, and all I could see was space and time. What I saw and heard were two totally different things. What I heard was a massive explosion happening to my far left that I couldn't exactly figure out – was it a mortar attack or was it a grenade that just went off? All the sounds started to blend together over time, but one thing that was clear was the fact that it definitely didn't sound inviting at all.

I had been stationed in Iraq for almost eight months and I promised I was over it. I didn't know when I signed up for the military to be a United States Marine that shortly afterwards I would be fighting for my life, day in, day out. Here I was in a land I'd never heard of, away from the world I had always known. As I stood there, I was thinking of a thousand what-if-worst-case scenarios, while my friend was standing next to me smoking a blunt. Again I heard myself say, "Let me hit that," but this time, I saw my arm stretch in his direction, with my fingers in prime position to accept his "green gift". I remembered the day like it was yesterday because, now looking back on it, it was the catalyst to the blind spot that started it all. Before that day, I was an avid believer that all marijuana users were personally anointed by the Devil and were on the express train to absolutely nowhere. Boy was I wrong, and I dare you to keep reading so that I can prove it to you.

Now, this was not my first introduction to the magical plant. The first time I tried it, I remember choking so bad because I pulled too hard. I got so sick off the first inhale that I promised myself I would never touch it again. Fast forward almost ten years, and here I was seeing if we could be friends again. See, in my mind, there was nothing this plant could do to alleviate the mind fuck I was currently standing in, so I figured the hell with it, as I put the brown blunt to my lips. I remembered inhaling, but being very cautious, because I didn't want a repeat of last time. I also remember not knowing if I was doing it right, not even fully understanding what I should have been looking for in the first place.

I let air flow straight to my lungs instead of letting it fill up my mouth, like I had seen it done in the movies. I blew the air towards the same dark horizon I had been staring at the entire time. Nothing was said between the two of us for quite some time. We finished in silence. We climbed down the bunker in silence, and we went back to work like nothing ever happened.

I waited for something, absolutely anything, to happen to justify all the things I had been preaching over the years, but couldn't seem to resist at this particular stage in my life. Would I turn into a crackhead now? Would my First Sergeant find out and have me kicked out of the Marine Corps? Did I smell like weed now? I asked myself all of these questions as I went back into my office (which was a wooden shack full of dust from a recent sandstorm that had just passed). I sat down on a stool eating Cheetos. I remembered thinking this was, HANDS DOWN, the best bag of Cheetos I'd ever eaten in my entire life. I felt like the crunch was extra crisp this time, like the cheese was this gourmet blend from an artisanal grower south of Paris. I don't know, maybe I just made that up, but I promise you, it literally was the best bag of chips I'd ever had. No lie!

I never told a soul what happened that night on top of that bunker while I was still in the military, for fear of possible repercussions. It was my last tour in Iraq, and I was on my way out. I didn't need anything standing in the way of me and my honourable discharge papers. After that night, things changed for me in unimaginable ways. I didn't have a negative reaction. I didn't start looking for harder drugs like the myths I had heard. Absolutely nothing at all happened, except an amazing bag of Cheetos and a great night's sleep.

We ended up leaving Iraq a couple of months later. When I got home, that's when I realised the real battle had just begun. I remember the first night home like it was yesterday. I had just showered after eating dinner. I still wasn't really used to sleeping without 20-plus other women in what we called a "squad bay", and all the added noise that I had become accustomed to. In my mind, EVERYTHING would go back to normal. Looking back on my naivety makes me laugh a bit. I laid down and got under the covers as usual. I got comfortable, snuggled up to my pillow and proceeded to drift off to sleep.

That was the precise moment all hell broke loose, literally. The first nightmare I had, I was riding along in a convoy, like I had done in the military, and all of a sudden we stopped abruptly. The door swung open and I saw this man without a Marine Corps uniform on. I quickly lifted my weapon to get ready to fire. I wasn't sure what was happening, but I knew this wasn't protocol and my fight-or-flight reflexes were 100 per cent activated, so I was going to go with my gut, shoot him and ask questions later.

None of that went to plan because, as I lifted my weapon that was slung across my lap, I was pierced in the neck by something very thin, but sharp. My reflexes lifted my right hand off the weapon to see what I had been shot with or by... was I bleeding? What is happening? Where is the Captain? All these questions were simultaneously going through my mind when my vision started to get blurry. I really started to panic then and I tried to jump on my feet to get better control of the situation. My plans and reality were two different things. My vision became blurry and all I saw after that was black.

I woke up hearing a language I didn't understand, but knew it was Arabic from our training. I looked at them and one of the guys lifted up a tiny needle and said, "frog poison" in butchered English. He then proceeded to lift me off the chair and I heard a crowd I didn't know was there, erupting with cheering and screaming. I wanted to run, and I definitely would have if I wasn't still under the influence of the drug. I was raised on this stage and as I walked up, I saw blood dripping off all sides of it. I couldn't see below, but my brain put two and two together quickly. I was then placed on my knees and, right before I thought some sexual abuse was about to happen, I felt my feet being bound and tied by rope. I was terrified, but military training taught me that you will either be a Prisoner of War (POW) or be killed, so I had mentally prepared myself for either, as soon as my eyes opened.

My feet were tied and I was flipped over, facing front side up of a guillotine. Blood dripped down my cheek, causing me to scream and this made the crowd wild with excitement. I heard a man say something in Arabic, as I was forced to watch my own beheading. The blade came down and, just as I closed my eyes to keep myself from actually seeing it, I suddenly woke up from that incredibly horrible nightmare.

I looked around and it was completely dark. I immediately felt my neck. It was there. I realised I was soaking in sweat – my blanket and sheets were wet. I got up, took another shower, changed my sheets and stayed up the rest of the night.

This happened every single night after that but it was drowning, setting on fire or death by sword. You think of it, and it happened in my sleep, eventually causing me anxiety just to even look at the bed. It got to the point where I was afraid to go to sleep. That caused anger and frustration that I couldn't get control of. I ended up going to Veteran Affairs (VA), which is supposed to be the place that veterans come to seek help after they are discharged. They gave me what I could only assume were horse tranquilisers, because I didn't have any dreams, but was completely incoherent the next day after I took them. I was at my wits end.

My family noticed the change as soon as I got home and my dad was the one that said, "Baby girl, how can I help? Something is clearly wrong." The problem was, I didn't know how he could help and I didn't know where to turn for the answers myself.

It wasn't until I was on the verge of a complete fucking meltdown that I remembered that eventful night in Iraq. I remembered it to be the last time I had slept well. I asked a friend of mine if he had any weed on him, because I had no idea where to start. I needed to ask someone I trusted.

He ended up supplying me with what I needed. I drove my car, feeling like I had 20 kilos of cocaine in my trunk. I was so incredibly nervous, yet the most I had on me was $20 worth. I got home and took a shower just to try to calm down and relax a little more. I put on music and turned the lights down low... don't ask me why, but I basically went through the same ritual as if I was about to have a friend come over, to get me in the mood. I rolled the sloppiest looking joint ever, because I had no idea what I was doing, and sat down on the couch. I made sure I stopped by the store and bought a lighter on the way home. I lit one end and inhaled in the other. I tried to remember how I had inhaled previously in Iraq, but couldn't remember if I was doing it right and, since I didn't have a mirror, I was just sitting there blind hoping I got it right.

The first thing that happened was my nose tingled like I had to sneeze. I twinkled it a few times to clear my nasal passageway and inhaled again. Then my shoulders began to fall and I hadn't noticed until I sat back that I was sitting straight up on the couch. I moved around until I found a comfortable spot with the joint still lit in my hand and, when I found it, I took another hit. I didn't have cable at the time so the only thing that I had in my DVD player to watch were rerun episodes of the TV show 'Martin'. I clicked play and when the theme song came on, I started bopping my head like it was a top 10 jam on the radio. I couldn't tell you which episode it was, because I was just staring at the TV and, for the first time in a long time, I heard complete silence.

The TV was on and the volume was up, but it just felt like someone had pressed mute on the channel for a moment. I suddenly felt the urge to lay down in bed. I hadn't had this feeling in forever and it was actually the opposite of before, when I used to be afraid to lie down. I would break out into a sweat just thinking about lying down, but this time was different. I didn't even finish the joint that night. I put it out, got up and laid down in the bed. I didn't know what to expect, but I didn't feel any anxiety as I laid there. I felt like my Tempur Pedic was hugging me ever so tightly, which I rather enjoyed. Next thing I know, I opened my eyes and it was light as hell outside. I heard three birds in the tree outside my window. I heard the garbage truck picking up my neighbours' trash and then drive off. I heard children walking to the bus stop, talking about their favourite video games. I looked at my ceiling literally trying to figure out what the fuck was going on.

Last time I looked, it was dark as hell and I had just laid down. Now it was daylight and it felt like a chunk of time was missing from my life. What time did I lie down? What time is it now? Did I have something to do today? OMG what happened to me last night? No one was with me so whatever happened I did to myself. Did I have a dream last night? That's when the other side of my brain acknowledged that I, in fact, did NOT have a dream. This made me sit up in bed and I noticed my body felt amazing, limber and refreshed. It shocked the hell out of me and I swung my legs over the bed to slip my feet into my house shoes. I stood up off the bed and looked down at my sheets, expecting to see the body sweat outline. To my complete surprise, it was bone dry. I gasped out loud. It literally took my breath away, because my brain started to put the puzzle pieces together.

I didn't have a nightmare or night sweats AND I got a good night's sleep. Can you imagine how monumentally game-changing that was for me? I wasn't dizzy or lethargic. I was ALERT and hungry. I didn't feel constipated, moody, or unmotivated at all. I felt like I could finally tackle the day and all the shit that comes with it. Like I could actually make it to the grocery store successfully today, as I thought about that time I sat in the parking lot for an hour before I just went home. This was incredible and I had to retrace my steps to see how this miracle had occurred. I walked up front to my living room and saw the half-burnt joint laying in the ashtray. I threw my hand over my mouth and whispered, "It worked."

I looked around like the secret service was going to come in any minute and kick down my door looking for major narcotics. I couldn't believe I didn't put it out before I went to bed, so I made a note of that and began to clean up my place. It had been weeks since I had the energy to do it and I did everything, from the ceiling to the floors.

The whole time I cleaned up, I kept saying to myself, "We'll see... let's see if it can do it again tonight." I did the same song-and-dance ritual that I had done the previous night, because I didn't want to jinx the results. I smoked again and again. I woke up the next morning even more refreshed and with no memory of having a dream. This was incredible and I didn't know how to explain what was happening, but I definitely knew something seriously was.

It took over 365 days for me to honestly come to the realisation that not only was the cannabis actually helping, but I also didn't crave crack, heroin, or any of the other hard drugs cannabis was allegedly a gateway to. I kept this a secret for so long and looked over my shoulder every time I saw my dealer friend, which was more often than I thought it would be.

I tried an experiment to sleep without it. As soon as I tried, the nightmares came back again. It was like they had never left and came back with such a vengeance that I became scared not to smoke before bed.

I was thriving in school and in life. For the first time in a long time, I remembered how good it felt and how I wanted to cry because I couldn't tell anybody about it. Not the VA, nor my friends and definitely not my very religious mother. I ended up excelling in school and transferred my credits from a nursing major to film. It was one of the most freeing things I had ever done and I didn't even get the idea until I had smoked one night in bed right before sleep.

I started to notice that my most inspiring thoughts came late at night when I was laying in bed. At the time, I didn't know that the cannabis was attaching to receptors in my brain, lifting me to a higher consciousness I didn't know existed without it.

Fast forward to me loving everything about film school and deciding after graduation that I was going to just go for it. I was going to go where I swore my whole life I wouldn't, which was the land of dreams in sunny California. I told myself that I was either going there for film or cannabis, and I would see which one the universe had in store for me when I got there. Like I always do when I make up my mind, I quit my job, sold my apartment, broke up with my boyfriend and hit the road by myself on this spectacular journey.

I had no idea when I left Atlanta that I would be driving from coast to coast by myself in the pursuit of happiness. I did the entire five-day journey with cannabis and music as my sole companions. I saw mountains, sunrises, sunsets and views I had only seen in movies. Things that I had previously taken for granted I was now fully able to appreciate, thanks to this amazing plant. I listened to one song 62 times in a row, just because I loved it and nobody could stop me.

When I finally arrived, my life would 100 per cent never be the same. I found a community of people just like me, of all shapes, sizes and colours, who had PTSD or some ailment that only cannabis worked for. For the first time since I left the Marine Corps, I felt like I belonged and that I wasn't wrong.

All the information I previously knew about cannabis was wrong and they were willing to send me in the right direction for the truth – the truth was way more interesting than the lie. If I never went to the military and went through my life experiences, I could have departed this earth still not knowing the magic and power of this plant. It's sickening the lies we have been told, but I'm just thankful that I am part of the growing demographic on the planet that knows the truth.

That, ladies and gentlemen, will forever be my blind spot moment.

Toniaamaka Chrisokere

www.theeverlastingtruth.org
Email: Godamaka@gmail.com
Facebook: Toniaamaka Chrisokere
Twitter: @Ctoniaamaka
Instagram: @ToniaamakaChrisokere

"We are all heaven citizens residing on earth for different purposes because it is problem solving that keeps us humans busy, that's why hell is shut forever, because everyone and anyone is RELEVANT."
Toniaamaka Chrisokere

Toniaamaka is a mother of four beautiful children who all have sickle cell anaemia. She's home schooled by God himself. This is one of the many challenges he created in her life, that he has used to transform her life, empowering her to impact lives. She is the founder of 'Everlasting Truth' and 'Hell Is Shut Forever', which she has been teaching through her online presence for almost three years now.

'Hell Is Shut Forever' is exclusive to her. She is taught and authorised by the everlasting living progressive ageless King, who created everyone and everything and loves all his creatures with an IRREVOCABLE love. That's why hell is shut forever, because everyone and anyone is RELEVANT.

Toniaamaka was the finalist for the Best Mother of the Year 2017 award for Women4Africa. Women4africa is an awarding body that celebrates African women who are doing amazing things.

She has been on Faith TV's 'Questions in the Heart' with Praise Funmi, to share her story and struggles. She is the only earth resident authorised to declare the second coming of Christ Jesus, to liberate minds from waiting for rapture and start living the victorious lifestyle already paid by Christ Jesus over 2,000 years ago.

She has been on 'Pauline Long Show' on Ben TV to share her story on the mental abuse she suffered. She is also a part of the panel for 'This Or That' on 'The Pauline Long Show' on Ben TV.

She studied secretarial administration after leaving high school and worked at Globestar, an oil company in Nigeria, which is a subsidiary company of Stolt Offshore. She has done several courses in counselling, parenting, business and customer service. She has also been a homemaker, caring for her young ones.

She is an eloquent woman and was chosen by the Children's Society in 2012 to help the council continue funding their services. Her input made a positive impact. Toniaamaka has also successfully spoken on behalf of Springboard for Women Returners to enable their funding to continue.

She has established a change no creature can revoke and has been raising awareness of her work to liberate minds from the many lies inherited from the previous generations through culture and religion. She is a game changer and has been delivered, without sentiments or apologies, ever since her self-discovery and acceptance.

Toniaamaka is a free spirit nobody can cage or limit, using her energy to navigate and attract what she believes she deserves, through helping the dreams of others become a reality by offering practical support.

Hell Is Shut Forever

Even though I had seen a revelation while in school about it, I did not see it coming as it came. It all happened like a movie. Hey, this is my own reality and I am extremely grateful that I am alive to write my story, which is a beautiful opportunity to reach out to many more who are waiting to hear my voice.

I have embraced my reality and that is the beginning of my victory. It empowers me to walk tall because I am living my talk. I am building a durable legacy that time will never prove wrong.

I am going to tell you about three major dreams which changed my life forever. One was before I was engaged, I saw myself carrying sick children up a staircase. I had this dream for four days. Each night I carried a sick child upstairs and I woke up worried, because I did not understand what it meant. I shared this dream with my room-mates and none of us understood it.

None of us knew that I would be a mother of four sickle cell children. This was even before marriage was on the cards. This dream came to be a reality in 2014, when one of my young ones was ill and could not walk up the stairs. I smiled as I made the connection, continued to carry them up the stairs to put them to bed.

Being strong is the only way I know to be. I am grateful for Great Britain having the NHS. Their doctors and nurses are all amazing and are always on standby in every crisis, I cannot thank them enough. It gets tough sometimes but hey... I have no reason to complain because my destiny has already been programmed. I cannot reprogramme it.

The second dream I had that was significant was in 1997. In that dream, I was walking with my supposed fiancé. I was already engaged when I had this one. Suddenly he saw another woman on the other side of the road and ran after her. I called him to come back but I woke up without him coming back to me. I wrote it down in my diary that I have since misplaced. Neither did I know that this dream would become my reality.

I did not know the woman in the dream nor did I see her face. It was later revealed to me that my church sister would play that role of betrayal in the lives of my young ones. I can remember helping her look after her youngest son during Sunday school, when she first joined our assemble, to give her a break.

One day at a women's meeting in church, she shared a testimony of gaining employment. Unbeknown to me at the time, it was obtained through my husband. The day of our baby naming ceremony, she looked very uncomfortable. She walked up to where I stood with my husband, congratulated us and told me she did not know he was married to me and that he was her boss. She continued to lie to the church, saying they had met in Nigeria, as if church people were deaf and blind. These are some of the evil things that goes on in SOME churches that prompted me to question many more things that I am glad I got answers for.

We all went to the women's meetings, ate from the same pot in the church and worshiped together. I thought it would be a stranger to betray me like this, but it was a woman I knew.

Before it all began, God had revealed this to me. When I woke up that morning I shared the dream with my husband and he denied everything. I am glad that I shared it with friends, who are living witness to my story that God had prepared me long before it all happened.

The third dream was when I was physically pushed out of the church by the pastor. Each time I wanted to come in, he would push me out. I also shared this with others before that too became reality. I was suspended from the church for telling the truth. Others were also suspended and I stood up for them, because it is just humiliating for someone who serves God to be suspended over an issue that can be addressed in a more reasonable way.

His first victims were a couple who were having issues and so were suspended. Who doesn't have marital issues? I called him and told him that it was humiliating. He said that's how it is done and they should be disciplined in order to learn. I told him that there are so many other ways to handle the situation without suspending them. Suspension is more like shutting heaven and humiliating them by excluding them from the congregation.

Their issue were made known – everyone knew that they were suspended because of marital issues. One brother was suspended, but this time nobody knew what he had done. His offence was kept confidential, but his suspension was made known to church workers. Nobody could challenge such injustices, as to why some people's issues should be exposed and some were kept confidential. I hate injustice with a passion. I asked God what the brother did that led to his suspension and God told me that he had committed adultery. I wept and kept it to myself as I watched the injustices and diabolic practices that were going on in church.

When the relationship between my ex-husband and the woman became open, God had instructed me not to say anything to her at all. I should respect her space and choice, which I did even though it was difficult for my young ones to share their dad with her children. It hurt them badly, but it was beyond my control, because it is divinity that's at work for the purpose of my existence to unfold.

The opportunity to voice my opinion was created by the pastor. I openly shared it during the workers' meeting when he wanted to also discuss my marital issues in the church meeting. I told him that is it good for the workers to know and understand what has been going on, because a lot was hidden from them. The atmosphere wasn't emotionally healthy, as there was always too much tension which we needed to clear. I had to speak out because, if we were genuinely a family, then every member deserved to be respected and accorded some form of confidentiality to feel free to share their burdens without fear of being suspended. They humbled themselves to open up for one's emotional well-being and security.

I was a threat because I told the truth that challenged him. He called me to his office and gave me a suspension letter, which I confidently collected and told him that, "Time will prove who is who, because I have done no wrong."

If God did not tell me that it was adultery the brother committed, I would not have known and if God did not also show me the diabolic practice in the church, I would not have known too. More so, I was a voice to those who could not speak out, because I wanted to end the injustice that was going on in the church for years.

What was hidden from me is that my story would change me into the powerful, fearless soul that I am today. I thought I lost, but I have recently realised that I gained and I am walking in power and authority daily, impacting lives to the best of my ability, joyfully. Writing this chapter will launch me into another phase of my life, which is exciting.

My challenges have transformed me into a responsible woman of integrity and dignity. I am loving my life. I am proud of whom I have become by embracing my pain, which is slowly becoming a profit for humanity, because I am the one woman teaching Hell Is Shut Forever.

This world is our home and one day we'll all die and make history like the previous generations, because the second coming of Christ Jesus is outdated information.

I never saw it coming. The revelation was given to get me. I was hurt, because this was not the type of family I wanted for my children. I wanted more than this for them. I never embarked on a marital journey to end up as a single mother but, to be honest, I've achieved more as a single mother than as a wife. I was bullied and abused to live in fear and self-doubt DAILY.

I was humiliated before my pastor and friends, at any given opportunity, by my ex. I developed all sorts of personalities to be the supposed 'perfect wife' until I lost my mind and who I was. When God came to my rescue and gave me a taste of FREEDOM to think and talk for myself, I could not settle for less. It was a treasure the Almighty Father gave me which is priceless.

My life journey is a hopeful one, because I am NEVER alone. All I hear from him is to be strong and courageous, remain focused and to refuse to be distracted, because life comes in phases and no painful phase lasts forever. It only lasts for a while, then births something beautiful.

What motivates me to fight are my young ones. I owe them everything good and will establish it before I leave this side of life. They will remember me and not be ashamed or live in fear. They will choose fairness and justice and walk away from where they are not appreciated without fear or apology, because that is the life they saw me live.

I tried to prevent being a single mother, but I had to face it when God taught me that he does not want me to be one of those people who suffer in a marriage trying to make it work, as we are meant to enjoy marriage, not endure it.

My revelations prepared me for all the challenges the universe sent my way. Pain activated my wisdom, hope, glory, strength, power, authority and direction.

I follow those I celebrate, not those I tolerate, and I don't hang around those who pity me. I hang out with those who inspire me. I now share my story with so much excitement. Sharing my experiences activates hope in others to walk away from abusive relationships or toxic atmospheres, and encourages them to embrace who they are, because they are here for a divine purpose. Embrace your own reality on time, because time is unsentimental, irreplaceable and very expensive to channel on those who are clueless of who they are.

From one generation to another, God creates problems to get our attention to solve his own problems, because it is problem solving that keeps us humans busy. I am home schooled by God himself through my challenges. I never went to Bible school, but pain drove me to pray until I could hear him myself. I am glad that I did not seek him in vain.

We worship the Everlasting Living Progressive Ageless King who is not dead or stagnant and cannot destroy us for being who he created us to be. We are emotional beings and express ourselves through our feelings. Our behaviour is a reflection of our emotions. I am an extraordinary soul and I only arrived at this conclusion by embracing the good, the bad and the ugly.

The above words empower me and make me feel special. I am pleased to be trusted to bring hope, healing, joy, laughter and progress to hurting souls. What an amazing privilege to influence lives with my pain, which I have been doing for three years now on Facebook.

Family and friends were worried about me, but God told me not to worry, that he is in control of all that concerns me. He programmed my life in a sophisticated way. Nothing beats a sound mind, that works and walks in purpose.

Disappointments taught me to expect anything from anybody. Being hurt for doing good taught me not to believe in karma. Pain made me question a lot. As a young girl, I did not run after other women's husbands, so why and how did I become a victim of this? I am blessed with many sisters biologically and spiritually and I did not have an affair with their husbands, so why? We are taught to believe that the blessings of God makes rich and adds no sorrow, so why all this pain?

I suffered abuse from a supposed Christian husband who told me daily that he will destroy me and called me all sorts of names at any given opportunity to make me live in fear and feel worthless. He brainwashed me to believe something was wrong with me, until I had a breakdown and ended up in a psychiatric hospital in 2007.

And to have four sickle cell children as well? It was just too much to bear and if that wasn't enough, I got suspended from the church for saying the truth. This was when church was my only outlet. They were the only family I had spiritually.

I was suspended and was made to sit at the back of the church like a criminal but HEAVEN knew that I deserved better and had done no wrong, but good. Heaven and earth remains my witness and will continue to vindicate me and command all that is due unto me.

I cried and God told me not to worry and sit where I was told to sit. I sat at the back of the church for over two years. I will never forget what God told me the first Sunday of my suspension. He told me, "CONGRATULATIONS," that I have won, and all they can do to me is make me sit at the back. He said my work has now been finished. People can only destroy what their eyes and hands can see and touch, but are powerless over what is hidden from them.

My suspension enabled me to create a platform on Facebook. I introduced myself as a warrior and princess of the universe, God's answered prayer. God told me that I am the only earth resident and 'Hell Is Shut Forever' is exclusive to me.

It is problem solving that keeps us humans busy, making everyone relevant, because some are here to create a problem, while some are here to offer solutions.

When God told me that I have finished my own share of work, I never knew that I was working. As I sat at the back of the church, God gave me a flashback of all I have been doing and told me that only a fearless, courageous, dedicated, faithful soul can deliver such a task excellently and only a generous soul can declare hell is shut forever. God told me that the everlasting truth is the truth that time can never prove wrong. My story is my trumpet and it is time for my voice to be heard. I should use my Facebook page to introduce who I am and leave the rest for him to handle. I never knew that this would be it.

I started sharing my story in bits, and faced all sorts of challenges and was called all sorts of names. Some said that I was an attention seeker, an antichrist, an agent of darkness, the name calling goes on... all of which God had long prepared me for. To others, I was airing my dirty laundry in public, but God told me that my story is my trumpet, that only he saw all that went on under my roof and I should sound it loud from the rooftops, that salvation is a free gift for all creatures.

I obeyed and that was how my healing began. Sharing my story has helped me heal. I now laugh when I talk. I do not cry and, if ever I shed tears, it is tears of joy and gratitude. I am an overcomer and I am happy.

Opening up has helped me impact lives and educate minds. I find peace and joy as I do so. It activated wisdom and healing within me. I wake up daily with a deeper revelation of who I am and to live and respect the existence of others.

Facing my challenges has helped me to grow into a powerful, responsible woman. Embracing my pain without playing the blame game has made me wise and stronger. Minding my business has saved me time and supporting others to pursue their dreams has gained me a larger family, because the success of others gets me excited and empowering them makes me more powerful.

Before I was suspended, church was my only outlet, but sharing my story connected me to more wonderful people who are more like family to me now. People reached out to me as they read my story and included me in their circle, inviting me out for programmes. I build family everywhere I go and embrace people as my brothers and sisters, because the everlasting, living, progressive, ageless King is our Daddy forever and loves us all with an irrevocable love.

My experience with the church has taught me to understand that when people are excluding you, they are indirectly teaching you that you deserve better WITHOUT them and you should use your precious time wisely, because time is expensive, unsentimental and irreplaceable. Whoever excludes you has saved you time and did you a favour. It is now your full-time responsibility to wisely use your time and resources to achieve something productive. Instead of begging to stay where you are not wanted, take it as an opportunity for expansion to progress for good and shut that door if it will demote you if left open.

The universe sends different people to play different roles in our lives for the best of us to unfold. If you have been genuinely fair to them, you stand a better chance in the long run, because memories are made not faked. That is why I encourage fairness and justice.

I was called back to the church workforce in 2016, but I already went far without them. I was impacting lives on Facebook and did not want to go and become a threat to anyone for saying the truth. I don't need to stay where I see evil, I don't need to become blind and deaf. People can lie to others about you, but they cannot fake their memory of you within them.

We depend on God's mercy daily. We all sin, disobey and annoy God in different ways. There is nothing like big or small sin. Sin is sin. Our thoughts and imagination are inclusive if we are to count sin by what is documented thousands of years ago and if hell is not shut forever, all sinners will end up in hell - which is all of us.

So, who is deceiving who? If we ask God for forgiveness, why can't we also admit we are wrong when we offend those who look up to us? Rather, we are suspended because of those who feel their title gives them an advantage.

For three years and four months, heaven was supposedly shut over me. What sort of suspension takes that long? The owner of heaven and earth kept promoting me from Facebook and I started appearing on television to share my story and to impact lives with my talent. Doors kept opening and, as I reached out to support others, I started discovering more beautiful things about myself. I noticed that I started loving myself more, using my powers positively to my advantage. Doing good makes me happy and keeps life traffic moving faster and smoother.

I did not return to the workforce, as I understood that my presence would become a threat. They excluded me, because I grew more and more powerful. The letter of suspension was enough for me to report them to the head office, but God taught me that he is the highest authority and it is his responsibility to sort me out, because he told me the truth.

Church is a support network, where people invest their time and resources, then get insulted and humiliated in return. In some places for their precious time, talent, and money. I walked away when I grew to understand that I AM THE CHURCH and fellowship is how I make anyone who comes my way in life feel, because God is not missing anywhere.

What you make of your story is your own responsibility. My pain has given me a voice nobody can shut. Without fear, I cut off whoever becomes a distraction in my life, because I am responsible for my words, actions and choices. I can never live in fear when heaven and earth is my living witness that my story is true and the motive is to promote fairness and justice.

Never look down on anyone or use your influence to abuse them with your powers, because you feel they can do nothing or that they are a nobody or that they are voiceless, because you are clueless of what they are destined for in life.

Destiny unfolds in mysterious ways. If you cannot offer any practical support for others, do not fight their destiny. Leave it to time, because anything that is not foundation fades. Why trouble yourself over what time can perfectly take care of?

This is my story. People will still share their story, even if they have forgiven you.

The people involved are good, but this had to happen for my destiny to unfold. Life is a movie – you have to choose which character to play, as tomorrow is mysterious.

My suspension from church helped to launch me to where I am today. I became a powerful woman who is walking in power and authority, impacting lives to walk away from abuse and toxic atmospheres.

Having four sickle cell children is a challenge on its own and the stigma that came with it is huge. People told me that

I must have done something terrible and God is punishing me by giving me four sickle cell children. Some even told me that if I had prayed properly, that prayer would have changed all the revelations I have mentioned. None of these people who said such things considered my children and the abuse I suffered from my ex. It was right before them.

If the church knew that this would be revealed one day, they would not have suspended me, but they did it because I was a nobody to them. If my ex could treat me in such a way with everyone a witness and get away with it, why couldn't they? I sat at the back of the church with my children for almost four years, for speaking out against abuse and injustices. It has become a story for the world to read and some of those churches that are promoting abuse and injustices have began to close down. They can come and fight me. They will never win, because the owner of the universe has my back and they all know that only God could have revealed it to me.

From one generation to another, the Creator creates problems to get our attention. Everyone who goes to work has to solve one problem or another to earn a living and whoever wants to get promoted is asking to solve a harder task.

My purpose in life is to raise awareness that his love for all his creatures is irrevocable, that is why hell is shut forever.

I have forgiven, but I am sharing my story to end the many atrocities happening in the church, which have been covered repeatedly – that's why the church stinks of iniquity. It is time to clean up and stop promoting abuse and injustice.

Tracy J Reid

www.tracyjreid.com
Email: hello@tracyjreid.com
Facebook: Tracy J Reid Coach
Twitter: @tracyjreid
Instagram: @tracyjreid

"Happiness is found when you find yourself."

Tracy is a certified life coach and has enjoyed coaching for over 15 years. She is a strong advocate for women being able to live their lives to the fullest, having a meaningful and fulfilling career, while also being available for their families. Tracy dedicates her coaching career to supporting busy women who are feeling the pressures of the daily grind and are ready to press the restart button on their lives.

Along with her coaching, Tracy has years of experience working within the corporate industry in the areas of PR, marketing and sales. She has brought together these skills, knowledge and experiences to support women who have an existing business and those who want to start their own, with the aim of creating a flexible career with a healthy work-life balance and clearly defined boundaries.

Some of Tracy's clients have commented on her ability to connect with them. This has enabled them to open up areas in their lives and past situations that they had never thought about previously, allowing them to lift barriers before unnoticed, which has unlocked a whole new potential for their progression.

She has a unique ability of infusing her energy and passion into people so they relate to their challenges as something which can be overcome with a gentle dose of self-belief and just the right amount of considered action for them to achieve lasting change, make clear decisions and take considered action steps. This allow them to achieve more joy and a deeper connection with themselves and others.

Tracy has been a guest blogger on Groupon, People Per Hour and *Choices* magazine, and has also shared her views on various other online and offline publications. In her spare time, Tracy enjoys working with various organisations as a volunteer, supporting young people who are keen to develop their personal and general life skills, some wanting to build their self-esteem and others wanting support in preparing themselves for a working career.

Tracy's coaching style is an empathetic, encouraging and empowering gentle navigation process. Supporting women to take a moment to focus on themselves in a self-love kind of way, through a series of daily practices and empowering rituals to make life-changing decisions and actions. The process taps into their feminine energy as a guide to follow through on their goals, reboot their health, recharge their energy and reclaim their lives.

I Want My Life Back

In life, there are times when a short, sharp, shock of reality is needed to get us to wake up from the slumber of a filtered view of our life, hidden and protected behind our blind spots to keep us safe.

For me, I have come to realise that when things get tough, I just keep moving so that I numb out the reality and feelings of the emotional pain or confusion of what's really going on. This is what I do, and did, during the year that my blind spot revealed itself to me. In a way that made me take a moment, to stop and take notice of what my body had been trying to tell me for many months.

My life had always been busy, lively, fun and exciting. I am a full-time working mother on a mission to change the world by helping women create wonderful careers and lifestyles that they love. Here I was living the life that I always dreamed of; a fantastic portfolio career, filled with all of the work opportunities that I could possibly dream of, from selling amazing luxury properties to being interviewed on podcasts, radio and TV shows. My own community of women was growing and I had a strong connection to who I was in the world and what my purpose in life was.

I loved socialising and organising events, which is how I got started with my networking group 'Stiletto Millionaires', for women who wanted to transition in careers or start a passion-based business. I organised meet ups and attended loads of networking events, as I enjoy meeting new people and discovering what made their hearts sing. This is where my passion for coaching really started to grow.

Most of my time would be spent networking or socialising with my girlfriends, hanging out with people that I had grown up with, like-minded people who shared the same interests as me whether it was through our kids' school, work colleagues, neighbours or any social events that I attended. I was always meeting people and inviting them to join me in my world of fun and excitement.

My friends would refer to me as being the "life and soul of the party". I would always be keen to throw a dinner party or celebration event for any occasion, mostly for the sheer enjoyment of organising it and seeing my people around me being happy. I have a really tight family and spending time with them on a regular basis is an important part of our family vibe.

Even with my fast-paced life of work and socialising, I can honestly say I loved every minute of it. Living in the fast lane was my way of being at that time of my life. I know now that it was my default mode that kept me safe. It prevented me from being fully with any emotional upset or traumas from my past taking hold of me.

Some people drink alcohol, take drugs or take up other addictions. I became a workaholic and busybody, which prevented me from seeing the truth behind my emotional pain and blind spot.

At the end of 2014, I remember looking back at that year after achieving so much personal success. Looking at my coaching certificate in my hand and smiling to myself, thinking, I did it, I actually did it. Everything that I set out to achieve in 2014 was achieved. Every goal, every desire and pretty much everything I had worked so hard to achieve was now my reality. I had a wonderful family, fantastic career and a thriving coaching business. You could say that I had it all and actually, it felt like I did. However, there was a deep feeling inside of me that something was not right. I couldn't quite put my finger on it, but there was something.

I went on through 2015, trying to keep up with the pace of life that I had created but truthfully, I was struggling. My energy waned, my body ached, I was becoming forgetful, unhappy at times for no reason and I just felt so exhausted all the time. However, I did not have the time to stop, pause for a moment and listen to my body. I just kept moving, living in the fast lane. There were always so many things that needed to be done that seemed to be more of a priority than myself. The busyness of my life stopped me from seeing the signs of my deteriorating health, until one fateful day when my blind spot was revealed to me.

However, at the beginning of February I started to notice I was feeling really tired, heavy-headed and dizzy most days. Then the headaches started to get more regular, which often turned into migraines that were difficult to shift and stopped me from being productive at work and at home. I was no fun to be around as all I wanted to do was lay down in a darkened room and close my eyes, which often led me to retiring to bed from early in the evening. The days seemed to all merge into each other, as this soon became a daily pattern of my life. I didn't accept invitations to go out with friends, as I could not predict if I would feel well at the time of the event. So I declined a lot of opportunities and stopped being social. It was easier that way, so that I did not let anyone down.

Through the exhaustion and ill feelings, I continued to keep going as I didn't have time to stop and investigate how I really felt in my body or talk to a doctor. There was always so much to do, whether it was for the kids, the home, work or my clients. I just kept thinking that how I was feeling must be normal, because there are so many women out there doing the same daily tasks as me and more, yet seem to be coping alright, even if they might feel a bit tired or stretched to capacity from time to time.

As the days and months went on, I started to feel worse, with the migraines occurring daily, with earaches, tiredness to the point where I would need to have a nap in the middle of the day and a general feeling of fatigue. I seemed to be getting colds and viral infections every couple of months that would not go, even with antibiotics. I felt weaker in my body every day. I was finding it hard to concentrate on anything and being focused or consistent with most things seemed to be challenging, not to mention the constant brain fog, dizzy spells and memory loss. Everyday tasks seemed like a massive challenge to do. I felt alone and confused as I couldn't even fully explain to anyone how I was feeling and, to be honest, most people didn't really seem to understand, even though they appeared to be sympathetic.

Most of those months seemed to be a blur. I can't remember most of what happened during that time. However, I recall visiting the doctors many times over a two-year period and receiving three doses of antibiotics to treat the viral infections that would not go, which would then come back some weeks or a month later. It was ridiculous how sick I felt, I just seemed to be getting sicker and weaker as the days and weeks went on.

With my health rapidly going into decline and with frequent visits to the doctors for blood tests and investigations without any conclusions, you can imagine how frustrating and stressful this was all getting. It was putting a strain on every part of my life. I used to have what seemed like my perfect life and yet I could not piece together why my life was so different now and, more importantly, what I could do to get my life back. Nobody was able to help me. The doctors didn't have a clue. I felt lonely, frustrated and even more upset.

People who knew me started to contact me to find out if I was OK, as they hadn't seen me for a while or heard from me. I even had social media buddies send me private messages to check in to see if I was OK. People started to notice that I was not present in the social circles any more, and I started to realise that there was something not right about this phase that I was going through. I was so tired most of the time – from the headaches, aches, pains and not sleeping well – that during the day there would be too much brain fog, lack of focus or just sheer exhaustion to get even the most basic things done in the home or at work. Somehow, I still managed to get through the days looking amazing, but feeling like crap inside, all while my body was crying out for help.

I had no brain space to plan ahead and organise any fun activities to do. Just getting ready to step outside of the house was a real effort for me and it would take me ages to lift my heavy head off the bed sheets and walk to the bathroom. This act involved so much brain activity and action that it could literally take a good half hour before I could even begin to start my day.

Now you might be reading this and thinking that this is not so strange or abnormal, if this is how you experience your days sometimes. However, what I came to realise is that it is not normal to feel like this constantly, day in and day out. I tried to stay being my normal, bubbly, happy self, but it was getting increasingly difficult to keep that up as my body was under pressure to maintain the spinning and busyness of my fast-paced life.

My body ached, my head ached and my ears ached. I felt like I had a constant head cold, with the glands in my neck being swollen causing neck pain and discomfort. The dizziness I experienced was also making me have vertigo, which panicked me even more. As time went on, it was all becoming unbearable. This feeling of constantly being tired, despite being in bed for many hours. I had been someone who could wake up really easily and refreshed with minimal hours of sleep. Now I would wake up and feel like a herd of elephants had been pounding on my head and my head felt so heavy, I could barely get out of bed with little to no energy at all.

There were subtle things I started to notice, like forgetting to do something indoors, or forgetting important dates for the kids' school activities. I guess it' quite normal to forget the odd thing, but it was becoming more frequent and definitely out of character for me.

I started to have anxiety attacks as I was afraid of collapsing on the street from the vertigo. Walking on the street sometimes made me feel unsteady as the ground felt unbalanced. When I mentioned this to the doctors, they gave me anti-sickness pills (needless to say, I never took them). Driving scared me even more, as my vision started to get blurry and I felt afraid to drive in the dark or travel to new places. So to keep my anxiety under control, I would only drive to local places and not take up any invitations further away if it would mean driving home at night-time.

It got to the point where I started to withdraw from more and more social events and not go out of the house unless it was for special occasions with people that I knew and, even then, it was a struggle to get myself dressed, ready and motivated to go out, but I would make the effort on a good day. I could not even find the energy for conversation in person or on the telephone, let alone go onto social media and interact with anyone on Facebook or Twitter.

Social media previously was my life and my coaching business thrived on it. Being in marketing, it was also one of my passions and social pastimes. However, during this time, it drained and overwhelmed me to the point where it was no longer enjoyable and I stopped opening the apps and stopped posting. I don't think I posted on my personal profile on Facebook for over a year during this time. I didn't have the energy for simple activities like getting out of bed, let alone writing a Facebook or Twitter post.

My friends and family started to notice that there really must be something going on, despite the fact that I still looked relatively OK. It was hard for people to understand how unwell I felt because when I went out of the house, I would wear make-up as my mask of how I really felt inside. It's amazing what a bit of make-up can do to help you cope with the outside world.

All of my symptoms persisted for over a year and then, one evening in April 2016, I had my awakening moment. It was a Sunday evening, when I decided to wash my hair. However, this day was not like any other wash day. As I shampooed my hair, I noticed that I could feel my hair in my hands in a different way. I felt my hair stuck to my hands through the shampoo, there were handfuls of my hair literally falling away from my scalp and into the sink. As I looked down into the sink and fully opened my eyes, I saw my hair, my beautiful, thick black curly hair was in bundles swirling around in the mixture of water and shampoo in the sink.

I felt sick to the pit of my stomach. I was scared and was shaking. I did not know how to stop my hair from coming out of my scalp. I continued to rinse out the shampoo and then towel dried my hair. I was afraid to look into the mirror, scared of what I might see.

Eventually I did look and the tears started to fill my eyes. My daughter was with me in the bathroom at the time and I did not want to worry her, so I held back from fully crying. She looked into my eyes and said, "Don't worry Mummy, your hair will grow back and everything will be OK." Bless her. Her words were very comforting and I wanted to sob my heart out, but I couldn't do that in front of her because it would cause her too much distress. I just agreed with her, put on a brave face and carried on drying my hair.

Inside I was so angry and upset with myself. I was telling myself off and literally screaming and shouting at myself in my head – how did you allow this to happen to you Tracy? What were you so busy doing that you didn't see the signs? What are you going to do now?

Although I had many questions in my head, there were no answers that came back at the time. All that I did know was that this was the sign that my body needed to see in order for me to listen. I found strength in myself that Sunday evening and was determined to find a way to get through this. I was always so good at helping others with their problems that I must be able to help myself. I must find a way to heal myself. I must.

I needed to get to the bottom of this and fast. I cannot accept what the doctors have said that my health was just a viral infection, old age, overwork, burn out or early signs of menopause. There had to be more to this and I needed to find out my own way. Nobody else was going to help me work this one out, I had to do it on my own.

I waited until I was alone in the bathroom and I had a good silent cry with tears streaming down my face. Looking into the bathroom mirror, I actually saw myself for the first time in a long while, looking like a sad, lonely and lost woman. I think this was the first time in months that I had really looked at myself and took in how different I looked and how much I had not seen the woman I knew myself to be, for nearly two years.

In that moment, I realised that I had lost nearly two years of my life to this debilitating feeling, and whatever it was, I had to find the answer quick. I was not prepared to be robbed of any more time. On my next birthday, I would be 50 years old. I have many friends who have already died due to unknown illnesses and hidden health complications. I was not prepared to be joining them any time soon.

In that moment, when I looked at myself in the mirror, I knew my mission was to do what the doctors could not do, to heal myself. If I got to the other side of my journey, I would share my story to help others find their own way to wellness. I wanted to stop feeling like this and I was not prepared to be fobbed off any more. If the doctors do not know how to help me, then I will have to find a way to heal myself once and for all.

I made a promise to myself that evening. I no longer want to feel like a woman 20 years older than my years and this is not how I intend to live the rest of my life as a woman. I needed to get myself out of this funk as quickly as possible. I am losing time, precious time. My life is precious and I am going to find out how to stop feeling like this, no matter how long it takes. I will not live the rest of my life feeling like this – no way! I am going to get my life back, no matter what.

I sobbed silently in the bathroom that night and after I was all cried out, I sat on the toilet seat with my mobile phone in my hand and started to ask Google for some help. Good old Google – always there to give you what you ask for. I was not prepared for the search results I read. I was amazed at what my research revealed to me. I had no idea that there were so many women that experienced hair loss and, to my astonishment, most of the blog posts, articles and forum posts that I read lead me to reading women's stories about their experiences with the Mirena coil and how it has affected them negatively with hair loss, blurred vision, memory loss, migraines, low energy, lethargy, the list continues. Practically all of the symptoms these women had, I had too! I couldn't believe it. At no time at all, was the coil a consideration, nor had it been mentioned to me by the doctors that it could cause so many side effects.

I was angry and so disillusioned with the medical system that I could barely sleep that night. I stayed up reading women's stories into the early hours of the morning. The first thing I did when I woke up was to book an appointment at the doctors to get the coil removed.

After some back and forth at the clinic, I finally had it removed a couple of days later and, despite the pain and discomfort, I felt like a new woman. I was so relieved that it was out and that my body and hormones could start to regulate themselves again.

Well, little did I know, hormones are not that simple – they wouldn't just go back to being balanced and supportive to my body overnight, that would take time. I also was not prepared for the other shift in my hormones by having the coil removed. It sent my hormones all over the place again. I have since found out that changes in a woman's body after taking any form of internal contraception can take anywhere between six months up to two years to regulate themselves again. Here I was thinking that it would be a quick process, that my hair would grow back and that my health would get back to normal. Nope. That was not to be the case. My health journey was to continue some more.

You see, the main reason why I was recommended to go onto the Mirena coil was because of my fibroids, which were still growing, and this was a way to shrink them. Well, I had a scan at the hospital at the end of 2016 and the fibroids were still growing and were up to five centimetres in size. This was really upsetting as I had already had major surgery – a myomectomy to remove the very large fibroids I had back in 2001. I had to have this surgery as the fibroids had caused huge complications when I gave birth to my daughter in 1999. I was advised that if I wanted to have more children, I could only do this if I had the surgery which I did in order for me to have another child. They still thought that it would be doubtful that I could have another child successfully unless I had a caesarian. However, I proved the medics wrong and gave birth naturally to my son in 2003.

The last thing I wanted to be told is that they have come back, they are large and they will continue to grow without some sort of medication to stop them from growing. This is what the doctor told me in November 2016.

This is when my search for alternative health and wellness therapies started to interest me and dominate my spare time. I am so passionate about women being able to heal themselves and find ways to combat debilitating illnesses that cause us to burn out, get ill or even die.

During Christmas 2016, I was having a restful duvet day and started searching Google for answers on how to heal fibroids naturally and how to regulate my hormones so that they would shrink naturally. I found more blog posts that led me to a 300-page ebook. I read it in one day and took loads of notes. This book and the advice it contained gave me hope. It listed out a plan and gave scientific information on why this plan worked. It made total sense to me and having the scientific evidence and data made it sound attainable for me to cure myself of fibroids and live a healthy, sustainable life.

This search led me to read a whole load of books on nutrition, health, well-being and spirituality, and how we can heal our bodies, master our minds and rid ourselves of illnesses and diseases. I have become so passionate about this subject and have found that through my research, daily rituals and sharing of my recovery, many of my clients and friends are interested in finding ways to integrate a new healthier supportive lifestyle before any serious ailments take hold of them.

I am glad to say that my new way of life fully integrates into my lifestyle and I am also on the road to recovery. I will never get those two years of my life back, but I am confident that I can live the rest of my life as the woman I came on this earth to be.

Through my studies, investigations and recent visits to various therapists over the last six months, I have found out that I've been suffering from adrenal fatigue and hormone imbalance from the coil, but the good news is, although it is a long process of full recovery, I am getting stronger every day. All of the symptoms I have been experiencing are classic symptoms of this hidden debilitating illness, which is known as adrenal fatigue.

Adrenal fatigue is a decrease in the adrenal glands' ability to carry out its normal function. It is commonly caused by chronic stress from any source (including emotional, hormonal, physical, mental or environmental) that exceeds the body's capacity to adjust appropriately to the demands placed on it by the stress.

If there was anything that I would want you to take away from reading this right now, it would be for you to start being observant with regards to your health and well-being, and seek to address any concerns you may have. Try to minimise stress, try to avoid getting burnt out or stressed out. Get as much exercise as you can and eat a healthy, balanced, nutritious diet. The process to repair and heal your body from adrenal fatigue can take up to two years and it involves a mixture of different practices, which I have used and have worked for me.

If you start to take action now and integrate some or all of these practices to heal your body, mind and spirituality, then you reverse or even prevent serious ailments from taking hold of your body. All you need to do is commit to a new healthy lifestyle and plan your daily routines and rituals to support you. Give yourself a good foundation of supportive coping and healing strategies for dealing with life's challenges, then you can draw on your reserves in times of need.

With all of the research I have done, there seems to be some key tools and techniques that will help anyone suffering from burn out or stress symptoms on your body and your mind. All of these are needed in equal doses in order to restore your energy, health and well-being.

As I have started talking about what has happened to me, more women have also started opening up and talking about their health concerns and changes in their bodies that were making them feel unwell. I am surprised and shocked by the number of women who are living with similar symptoms, silently trying to cope and not doing too well at it, which turns to depression, loneliness and anxiety. Often these women are misdiagnosed and given prescription medicines to relieve symptoms, which invariably creates even more problems as it is hard to pinpoint the exact root cause to the long, debilitating, silent suffering.

Doctors need to educate themselves about illnesses such as adrenal fatigue and other autoimmune disorders to catch the signs early in patients, so that treatment can be suggested. If these illnesses go on for a long time unnoticed, they can become life-threatening.

I want to help women find their own path to wellness and support them on their journey, so that they do not lose years of their lives and miss out on enjoyable moments with their family, friends and loved ones.

During my health recovery, there were a few principles I adopted to get to the other side of wellness and they are simple, practical, daily rituals and health choices. Even if you are not feeling any of these symptoms, lifestyle changes are always a good way to feel good.

It is no surprise that women are feeling more stressed out than ever, as we take on so many roles in life, from daughter, wife, working mother, etc., all of them require so much of us. It is important that women manage their well-being and health during these highly charged modern times. Women need to find coping strategies to help deal with daily challenges, to take the pressure off by adopting some practices that allow them some down time and important 'me' time.

There were many things I did to get my life back. I have listed the main steps that I took to reclaim my life, which I hope will help you or someone you know who may be going through similar health challenges.

Mindset Shift

It is essential to have a healthy mind if you want a healthy body. Filling your mind with positive self-talk and positive affirmations is a daily practice that helps build up self-confidence and faith that you have the ability to be, do and have anything that you desire.

Find a few affirmations that resonate with you, write them out on post-it notes and stick them up in places in the home, at work, in notebooks or even in the car.

The environment that you are frequently in needs to be uplifting and motivating. There were people and places that I found made me feel uncomfortable and stressed. I made it my responsibility to avoid those places and people as much as possible to protect my feelings. If I did find myself in conversations or situations where I would feel slightly uncomfortable, then I would find a way to communicate with how I was feeling so that the feeling is not left with me. Over time, I learnt how to not be triggered by the behaviour of negative people.

Mindfulness

There is a reason why everyone is talking about being more mindful. This practice can literally change your life and your way of being for the better. You can practise mindfulness in many ways and it can be easily integrated into your lifestyle, no matter how busy or hectic your schedule is. This can be anything from meditation, taking up a hobby that helps you to be still and focused on the task at hand, or for you to do an everyday thing in a mindful way by being truly present. I enjoy cooking and this helps me to relax and be mindful by following the recipe, preparing the meal and finally sitting down with the family to enjoy together.

Meditation

I have a daily practice that keeps me grounded and focused, which fits into my lifestyle and has brought me immense joy and a sense of calm. I now cannot imagine life without meditation. Find a practice that works for you and be committed.

Exercise Routines

I have never been a gym bunny and found it difficult to take up any form of exercise with enthusiasm and consistency, as my energy wanes easily. However, I found something that I love doing, that is easy, does not need any equipment, I can do alone or with company and is also free – walking. I absolutely love walking and I have integrated a weekly mindful walking practice with my girlfriend. We do a 10k walk every Sunday, followed by a delicious, healthy brunch wherever we end up.

I have also recently taken up yoga. There are many forms of yoga and, again, finding the right variation that works for you and your body is key to your enjoyment of this wonderful practice. Yoga helps me to focus on being present with my breathing and the poses. My other exercise love is hula hooping with my power hoop. Not only does it make me feel good, but my body is starting to shape up and look great.

Even 10 minutes of a hula hooping workout is enough to make me feel good.

Diet & Nutrition

I started my new healthy living regime to treat my fibroids with a liver cleanse, and ended up with a completely changed diet and lifestyle. This totally changed my whole relationship with food. If you have any food intolerances and need to find a way to replace those food groups with food that nourishes your body without causing discomfort, then doing a liver cleanse or detox is a great way to reboot your system. My new diet consists of mainly gluten-free and dairy-free foods to help reduce inflammation in my body and increase my energy.

I also do not eat meat by choice and I am allergic to nuts. I replace protein with eggs and spinach-rich green smoothies. My diet is limited to food groups my stomach can tolerate, therefore, I could be missing out on key vitamins that my body needs, so I take supplements daily – vitamins A, C, and D, folic acid, iron, multivitamins and probiotics. My body is much happier and so am I.

Sleeptime Rituals

This is fundamental to the recovery process. The cells in your body replenish and repair themselves when your body is resting in sleep mode, so you need to allow your body this special time at the end of the day to heal and nurture itself.

If you imagine, not getting enough sleep and not allowing your body to switch off is like not ever turning a computer off and allowing it to 'shut down' properly. I am sure you have seen the warning message on your computer screen when you have not shut down properly or you get a warning message when the battery life on your laptop is running low. Well, your body will throw out warning signs too. You need to stay alert and learn to read the signs your body sends to you, so you can properly shut down before your energy source burns out.

Sleep is fundamental to the body's healthy cell growth and development to perform on a day-to-day basis to the best it can. It is the one thing that human beings cannot and should not be in deficit of in order to live a healthy life.

Holistic Therapies

During my health recovery, I worked with many wonderful holistic therapists who helped my healing process using various forms of therapies from life alignment, rebirthing, reflexology, hypnotherapy, angelic reiki healing, chakra cleansing with crystals to acupuncture. All of these therapies have brought something different and uniquely special to my overall well-being. Modern therapies of this nature deal with the cells and muscles in your body to restore balance and harmony to your well-being from the inside out.

Decluttering To Heal Your Life & Mind

A daily practice that helped me to clear emotional trauma and upset from my mind was writing a journal in a notebook. I would write how I felt about the events of the day, whether happy or sad, as this allowed my feelings to flow out of my head and body onto the paper, leaving my body and mind free to think new, more empowering thoughts.

I find that decluttering the home makes me feel lighter and clearer, as everything is organised in its place and I can find exactly what I need, when I need it. This reduces the need for panic and anxiety when things are misplaced.

Decluttering enables you to let go of the past and welcome the new. Getting rid of old unwanted items is so liberating and frees up space for lots of new items and exciting experiences to come into your life.

I found it useful to write in my journal in the evenings, when I could reflect on the day's events. It was also an opportunity to record events and express my gratitude for all of the wonderful things that had happened during the day.

There are so many daily practices and rituals that can help us to change from the way we are, to the way we want to be. My journey has now begun and I am grateful that my blind spot was revealed to me, so that I could recover and reboot my health while I am young enough to make the changes to reclaim my life and be the woman I came here to be.

We all have 'blind spots' in our lives, often life is challenging and we are thrown curve balls. However, while we are busy keeping up, we must start to take notice of what is happening right in front of our eyes to ourselves and our loved ones.

I would not want you, or anyone you know, to experience the kind of blind spot that causes a shortened life or causes someone to miss out on valuable, enjoyable years, as I have experienced with my health. I urge you to be more aware of any signs and practice going inward to listen to your body and look out for those warning signs, find your own path to wellness and live your life to the max.

We are all on this earth for a reason. It is our responsibility to live a long and healthy life so you can be the person you came here to be. Remember to have fun, enjoy your journey and remember to learn lessons along the way.

Much love, light and laughter.

Valerie Campbell

Facebook: The Secret Vibe
Twitter: @TheSecretVibe
Instagram: @TheSecretVibe.co.uk

"That which does not kill us makes us stronger."
Friedrich Nietzsche

Valerie Campbell is a love attraction coach who specialises in the law of attraction. She is the author of *She's Got That Vibe*, which teaches women how to attract the man of their dreams by the intentional use of their positive vibes.

Valerie's drive is to help women learn how to develop and stand firm to their own ideals by being strong, clear and true to herself through an understanding of how powerful she truly is.

Having suffered an abusive upbringing, particularly at the hands of her father, Valerie didn't learn healthy ways to interact with men, which caused her to attract unhealthy relationships. She has learned to manage her relationships through a combination of learning, gained through her trials, errors and successes. Valerie has an innate desire to give back and empower other women.

Valerie is also a serial entrepreneur and life enthusiast. Born in London to parents of West Indian origin, she is the second eldest of 11 children, thus she learnt responsibility at an early age. At age 18, she set up her first business in Barbados, selling jeans and T-shirts, sourced from her travels around the world, from places that included England, Venezuela, Saint Lucia and New York. These experiences increased her confidence enormously.

From there, Valerie worked for the London Council Refuse Collection Service for 10 years. As the only female manager in a 120 male-dominated environment, she learned, from friendly talks with her 'boys', as she fondly calls them, the inner workings of the male mind, as well as the mistakes women keep making.

She is also an avid student of personal development from such leaders as Oprah Winfrey, Bob Proctor, Marianne Williamson, Esther and Jerry Hicks, Miguel Ruiz and Michael Losier. Her favourite business authors include Robert Kiyosaki, Napoleon Hill, Dan Kennedy, Zig Ziglar and others. She is a prolific reader who continually seeks to improve herself!

Valerie's personal growth continues through the word of God, the study of mind, power and the law of attraction, which has been the foundation for most of her adult life – as well as founding her own internet marketing consultancy and a limited partnership company. This has left her greatly empowered to continue her spiritual journey and to inspire both men and women to fulfil their spirit's purpose and destiny.

Eve's Story

Once upon a time, there was a young girl named Eve. She was 8 years old, a sweet young girl of West Indian parentage. Eve often wore her hair in neat afro plaits or sometimes cornrowed in a range of styles, finished with a beautifully tied ribbon. She was the Cadbury girl with a dark and pretty complexion, smooth as buttermilk, with a very shy smile.

Eve's favourite pastime was to read. Oh my, did Eve love to read! Even though she was the fastest runner in her class and had the option to be very competitive at playtime, you would most often find her tucked into a corner alone, reading a book. At that time in her life, she had an insatiable appetite for fairytales.

Home was no different, you'd find her in her favourite secret place, stretched out behind the length of the three-piece settee, as it formed a cove against the wall where she would cocoon herself. Eve must have read every single fairytale out there. Her favourites were the Ladybird books that had the most amazing imagery bringing the stories to life. Stories like 'Cinderella', 'The Princess and the Pea', 'Three Little Pigs', the list went on! Then, when she was finished, she'd go on to the tales of Hans Christian Anderson or the Brothers Grimm, always eagerly onto another.

Most of the tales Eve read were of characters out to seek their fortune, while overcoming some sort of adversity, whether it was a troll under a bridge wanting to eat them, or a giant trying to get Jack's bones to make bread. Brave Rapunzel who let down her long hair so she could be rescued, Cinderella who endured the abuse of her stepmother and sisters or a princess that kissed a frog, who then turned into a prince, and let's not forget Little Red Riding Hood and the Big Bad Wolf! But what really made her beam inside were the happy endings. They would always end with her sighing as the prince found his princess and whisked her off to his palace where they would live happily ever after! Eve would often daydream about being a beautiful princess and being swept off her feet by a handsome prince.

Outside of the fairytales, her reality was quite different and yet there were similarities. Eve was the second eldest of a large family that would eventually have 10 siblings, five girls and five boys. It was a large home, often noisy, crowded and lots of sibling rivalry with very little privacy. However, she did have other secret places of escape; the quietness of the airing cupboard with the boiler to keep her warm, or the privacy of the bathroom with her back against its locked door.

Both her parents were strict, her mother a bit softer, but her father, very stern! In fact he was the Big Bad Wolf, tall, dark, cold and snappish! She felt the love from her mother, but not from her father. He never ever told her he loved her, in fact, he would curse her. He never had a good thing to say. He would call her and her sisters, 'watless' (West Indian for worthless) and 'nasty'. He would say that if they were to ever get married, the doorbell would ring and there would be their husbands saying, "Here, take back your nasty bitch!" Eve couldn't remember a single word of affirmation, praise or expression of love from her father. It was all part of the norm.

Eve and her sister, being the eldest, had to take on the majority of the chores. There wasn't a washing machine, so it was a normal sight to see Eve and her big sister hunched over the bathtub washing masses of clothes by hand. Then of course, there was the ironing... 13 shirts pressed in consecutive fashion every Sunday! The house was a large six-bed and they would also sweep the stairs from top to bottom with a brush and dustpan, wash the dishes and make the beds – they both operated like shift workers.

It was a Roman Catholic household and one where freedom of expression was definitely not encouraged. Children were told to be seen and not heard. To their parents, the word 'no' simply did not exist. They would get beaten with a belt for getting things wrong and, for anyone familiar with West Indian households in the 70s, this was a regular occurrence.

Early in the morning, as she lay in her bed, she would hear her dad getting ready for work and then leave at 6am. Bliss! Her mum would wake up around the same time and prepare him a packed lunch, usually of bakes (also known as fried dumplings) that she'd cooked from scratch and fill with fried or scrambled egg. For Eve, it was a pleasant smell as it wafted into her dark room that she occupied with four of her sisters.

When her dad would return from his work at Buckingham Palace, every child would scatter from his dark and opposing presence. They would leave whatever they were doing, as if to literally disappear into the walls in their bid to be quiet. If he happened to come home and catch them unawares when they were all present and having fun in the sitting room, each child would make a hasty retreat to do their homework, just to get away from his dark, foreboding energy.

Yet, despite this, Eve was a happy child! It was all she knew and so she continued to do what made her feel joy inside. In her dreams, she'd defy dragons, be rescued by

Prince Charming, kiss frogs or be woken by a kiss in her disguise as Sleeping Beauty. In her innocence, Eve didn't know what real love felt like from a man; in fact, she didn't know what it looked like.

One day, aged 11, Eve was upstairs making the bed. She was merrily humming to herself until suddenly she could hear his feet on the stairs. Her voice caught in her chest, as she could feel the Big Bad Wolf approaching. He never had anything good to say and then there he was, looming above her, tall and dark against the doorframe. He looked down at her, calling her by her name that all her family called her, "Alaeve, you haven't done that right! Fix that side of the bed again!" he barked as he pointed with an accusing finger. He always criticised anything she did.

Eve responded, "Yes Daddy," as she hurriedly flew to the corner of the bed. Abruptly, he walked quickly towards her and instinctively she held up her arm to cower from the blow she felt surely would come, but instead she felt a different sensation. The silence seemed to stretch out endlessly, although in reality it was seconds. What was he doing? It was as if a bird were flapping its wings, trying to escape, but was caught. It was her voice trapped... and the bird, as her psyche registered what was happening, silently screamed deep inside, "Stop it Daddy... stop it! Daddy, no, don't touch me there. I'd rather you beat me than touch me like this! Can't you see I'm scared? You're supposed to be my father!"

As he pressed his foul mouth onto her, she felt so dirty and so unclean. Any notion of feeling like a princess vanished that instant. From that day, her father began to inappropriately touch her. Her world up until that point had looked pink; it was now a murky grey.

She felt she didn't have anyone to turn to. When Eve had encouraged her elder sister to make a complaint to Mummy, having observed Daddy creeping into their room in the dead of night and hearing her sisters' whimpers, her mum had responded, "Let's ask Daddy if this is the truth." Mum was 20 years younger than dad, and asked him as opposed to confronting him. As you probably would have guessed, he denied it. To her young mind, it appeared to her that no action had been taken to protect her sister. So what was Eve to do? Look after herself, rely on herself, escape from him herself.

Eve felt like she was continuously on the run and so, in defence, she made herself as invisible as possible by wearing baggy clothes. Little did she know that she'd also become invisible to herself. She didn't see or embrace her body as it grew into womanhood – into a beautiful princess.

As she developed as a teenager, she knew her figure was attractive, because at her convent school, the girls would always comment and compliment her on her curves. The only problem was, to her it was a curse, because Daddy knew it too. To top it off, her face was covered in acne; she was on the run, not just from her dad, but from her own internal self because she felt so horrible.

She dreaded going home, and as usual, she would step out of her uniform, hang that up and put on her 'cloak of protection'. She didn't want Daddy touching her sensitive growing breasts again or pressing himself against her as he entered her room at night or speaking to her in a way no father should speak to his child, asking her if she knew what a clitoris was. Shudders. Her mind was always alert, never at rest, so as to never be left alone in the same room as him. For the early part of her teenage life, she felt like she was constantly on the run. Ironically, being the fastest runner in her class didn't save her! So she and her sister protected themselves as best they could. She tried to cover her sister's back, as best she knew how, as she knew she had it worse.

One day, her mum announced for the first time ever that she was travelling to the Caribbean. Eve was in knots with fear! You see, up until that point, it was her dad who would travel to the Caribbean for a period of six weeks every single year, which meant utter freedom and happiness for Eve and her siblings, yet here was Mummy saying she would leave her behind with this monster! She felt like Mum had just locked her in a cage with a wild animal with nowhere to hide, exposed and vulnerable like prey. In her head she screamed, who will I hide behind?! She imagined weeks of horror. It would be a wide open playing field, with Mummy gone who would be there to protect her? He would have full control of the house! Eve was desperate. She got on her knees that night and prayed hard. "God, please take this away from me, please protect me, please protect me." Every night she prayed. As if by magic, her mum announced prior to her departure that her cousin would be coming over from the Caribbean to study to be a doctor. He would be staying at the house in the time that her mum would be away. They had never had a family member stay over ever. Hurray! Her prayers had worked!

Her father never tried to touch her in that period of time, apart from the odd slimy 'knowing' glance! She guessed for fear of being caught and so it stopped. Her cousin ended up staying for six years.

As the years went on, Eve, now an adult, never bolstered up the courage to confront her father about his behaviour. However, her younger sister and brother did! This caused him to up one day and return to the Caribbean for good, leaving Mum behind to raise the children.

Eve did not know a father's warm and nurturing love; she just knew she envied it. She didn't know how to relate to men in a healthy way within a relationship – she didn't have a father figure who exemplified this. When it came to matters of love, all she knew was what she had learned on the TV and from her parent's example.

Nowhere in her mind was the expectation that she would come to such harm at the hands of her own father, whose role should serve as protector. You see, a girl first learns how to receive love from a man based on the standards set by her father.

It was no surprise then that, in her early 20s, she attracted a man in her life who physically and psychologically abused her. He spoke abusive words to her such as, "You're like a toilet," but she tolerated it, despite knowing it was wrong. She stayed because it was familiar to her, she had seen her mother stick it out and so thought it was the right thing to do; that she was exhibiting loyalty, no matter what. She had not realised that she'd been taught low self-esteem through the example of her parents.

Eve's awakening, as it were, would begin at the age of 23 as she began counselling. This was prompted by a leaflet found one day at the foot of her front door. The contents of it resonated with her deeply, as it offered services to young adults who had been abused. She knew she had to make the call.

Through counselling, Eve came to several understandings that, because she was taught not to express her wants as a child, she was thus unable to stand up for herself, even as an adult. Her voice remained trapped and so this carried through into her relationship. She tolerated abuse, because it was 'familiar' to her. She attracted an 'emotionally unavailable' man, because her father was of this disposition. Eve's biggest insight was that, even though she was 'lost' (i.e., invisible to herself) she hadn't lost her value! Much like in Luke 15:8-10 in the Bible, where it makes reference to a woman who swept her house clean in search of a coin – even though it was lost, it hadn't lost its value, but had lost its usefulness.

Eve wanted to be 'useful' and learned that she couldn't be if she wasn't expressing her wants and desires. She learned that her opinion was just as valid as anybody else's. As she began to express her voice that had been suppressed for so long, her self-esteem crept up, in small steps and in the right direction. Eventually, the abused woman who'd attracted that abusive man no longer existed and, eventually, neither did the relationship. What remained of their union was a beautiful baby girl.

Eve was sending out a vibe – a vibe that was attracting men who were also of a low vibe, who also had low self-esteem issues. Eve was to later learn a law, through her personal and spiritual development studies; known as the law of attraction that states 'that which is like unto itself is drawn'. This would form the lens through which she saw the world.

Eve's self-esteem grew to the point that, on her career path, she attracted a job in which she would manage in excess of 120 dustmen. She was the only female! She continued her work on self-love by reading a plethora of personal and spiritual development books which helped to heal her from the inside out, bringing out what was in the dark into the light. God's universe had placed her in a sea of men – what other learning ground could be more appropriate as a medium to learn and enhance her self-esteem in relation to men and how they view women in the context of relationships? Eve's learning 'pool' would have her swimming there for 10 years, until she was strong enough to reach the shore and stand on her own two feet! Not incidentally, she began to attract higher-quality men!

Now, I imagine you've already guessed that the Eve I speak of is myself...

I don't know what your story is, but for all the women out there who know they're not walking in the best version of themselves and getting the best out of their relationships, then my personal insights gained through my story are here to serve you.

My beliefs created a tower around me to protect the little girl inside. I had become a Rapunzel of my own doing. However, as I got older, I saw the shackles it had on me, causing me to interact with others in an unhealthy and limited way and I desperately longed to escape its hold on me.

I felt inner shame – this feeling of unworthiness and not feeling 'good enough' permeated everything around me. I felt if people could truly 'see me', then no one would really see me as worthy of connecting with. Thus, at that time of not feeling like a princess, I attracted a relationship to validate that feeling of low worth. That vibe I was projecting!

The 11-year-old created that story to protect me and I am so grateful for her strength and wisdom. However, I had to let her story go and replace it with one that served me going after my wants and desires, making me useful and fulfilling my purpose! You see, in order to connect with others, you must first have the ability to connect with yourself. This is necessary in order to be seen, to be visible... and to do this, we need to be vulnerable.

You are the common denominator of your relationships and every relationship you attract is based on how you feel about yourself. We are all energy and your vibe attracts like vibes by way of circumstances and people that support the feeling you have of yourself. If you have low self-esteem, then what will you attract?

How you see yourself in your mind's eye is all important. The universe will always validate how you see yourself by giving you experiences that match that. It is our beliefs that determine what you see and, in my case, it was that I was dirty and unclean.

When you believe you are dirty and unclean, how do you interact with others? Are you open and approachable, or do you hide and stay invisible? You see, even though I'd grown up, I was still controlled by that subconscious belief that I had about myself, so I was attracting men and circumstances that would validate that belief.

As I began to clean up what I believed about myself, I saw myself differently. In changing my story to that simple idea that 'I'm worthy', the universe conceded to me by giving to me that which matched how I felt about myself.

You will only attract more of how you feel about yourself

When you're in darkness, how you do expect others to see you, if you cannot even see yourself? You must have compassion and be kind to yourself. You cannot practice compassion with others if you cannot first practice it with yourself. Compassion leads to self-connection, your connection leads to your authenticity, thus your ability to connect with others.

When you shine a spotlight on yourself, you become visible to yourself and so others have no choice but to see you! Don't let your vulnerabilities hold you back. Have the courage to be open and vulnerable, and tell your story with your 'whole heart'.

FORGIVENESS is the key to heal your vulnerabilities. If you do not forgive and clean up your energy (your vibrations), you will be forever kept on a perpetual circle of attracting like energy in your life to reflect how you feel about yourself.

Forgiveness is the crux of dissipating all pain. Forgiveness for me was not condoning or saying that what my father did was OK. It was about taking a stand to not be willing to carry the weight of the pain any more, thus nullifying its power to permeate and affect all areas of my life.

It is the willingness to let go of the control of who you think you 'should be' in order to accept yourself as you are.

That is embracing your imperfect and vulnerable self in order to connect with others. It takes courage to be vulnerable! Being willing to be vulnerable is a measure of courage. It is not a weakness, as some may think. It is the route to your authenticity. It is the springboard for freedom, creativity, joy and belonging!

I want you to approach life feeling worthy. I want you to approach anything with boldness, feel deserving and have that sense of worthiness spill into every area of your life. I want for you creativity and joy! Not just in relationships, but in how you interact with everyone you connect with.

The most important relationship you have is the one you have with yourself.

Truth is, I am a princess, I always was, I just locked her in her tower and lost sight of her. Now that I've forgiven and had compassion with myself, I have set her free! We are all princes and princesses. Find your worth within you and your princess or prince, and certainly your purpose, will find you!

Valerie Kudjoe

Email: artyval@yahoo.co.uk
Facebook: Valerie Kudjoe
Instagram: valeriekudjoe

*"And we know that all things work together for good to them
that love God, to them who are the called according to
his purpose."*
Romans 8:28 KJV

Valerie is a co-author and proofreader who has worked as an administrator for over 20 years. She has also worked in event management; organising weddings, birthday celebrations, conferences and other events.

Valerie has a BA Honours in Fine Art and has gained certificates in Business Administration. She has a very good command of the English language and is regularly sought as a proofreader and editor for books, magazines and other literary productions on an international level.

Valerie has a passion to help young women be confident and achieve great things in life. She has worked for charities, delivering projects for teenagers providing educational support through music, dance, drama and media.

Valerie currently juggles her time between office work, being the wife of a pastor, mother of a young son and working with teenage girls at the church she attends, mentoring them through their formative years. As vice-president of the church's women's department, she engages in many other duties, including counselling, teaching and encouraging the women, helping them to identify their gifts and the ways in which they can utilise them to become all that they were created to be.

In her rare, precious moments of spare time, Valerie enjoys travelling, reading and photography.

The Artist and the Businessman

Artists never make any money until they're dead, the artist had heard that a million times. Well they definitely make a lot more money posthumously, people usually conceded after she had listed a number of rich ones who were this side of the grave.

While on a BA Honours Fine Art degree course, the artist was excited to receive an offer to paint images which would be used for greeting cards. Great! An opportunity to make some extra cash, because that student loan lasted as long as it took to walk to the bank. With this offer, she felt like a real artist receiving her first commission and not just a mature student, which she was.

She knew she was a mature student when she walked into the studios at the university and was greeted at the door by a 10-foot high sepia painting of male and female genitalia 'in the very act'. Trying to hide her shock, disgust and the realisation that she had led an extremely sheltered life, she hurried past the piece thinking, maybe Daddy was right after all. Her father, a preacher, had refused to allow her to go to art school at 18, because he didn't want them to 'defile' her mind. So she had just taken the first job she could get as a cashier in Peckham Sainsbury's.

The 'commission' to paint the images for greeting cards came from a businessman, whom, it was assumed, was a person of integrity and good morals. He was tall, dark, handsome and a smooth-talker. He claimed to be very successful in business, had all the trappings of success and it was widely accepted in his circle of influence, which she was familiar with, that this was indeed the case.

He presented a convincing argument, more like a charming rhetoric, telling her how he had been looking for a good artist for some time who could take on the project to launch his new range of fancy greeting cards. Well, his search had ended with her – she was the one! To the artist, it was akin to being on X Factor with Simon Cowell telling her he thought, "She was special!" The businessman's soft tone stroked her ears telling her, "how good we could work together in business" and how profitable it would be. It would be silly not to accept.

The proposed fee for each image was fair, considering this was her first real venture into business and the artist had no reputation to speak of. The amount of images he was suggesting was in double figures. She could make hundreds if not thousands of pounds because it was ongoing and, as the businessman said, "people always want greeting cards". No only making money when she's dead here! She was going to be a rich living artist! It sounded ideal. They shook hands. He gave her his business card and his private mobile number. He even gave her a few pounds to buy the materials she was going to use to paint the images. They agreed a date for her to start and even the method of payment. There was no written agreement.

The artist set about collecting items and taking photographs to create compositions to paint. Relatives, friends and anything that caught her eye were utilised to make up the pictures he had requested. Some people had no idea they were being immortalised on canvas – well, paper, but good-quality paper. She also typed out her invoices for each completed painting at the agreed rate, and felt a sense of satisfaction that she was earning money doing what she loved.

Several images later, she was presented with some glossy greeting cards with her amateur images on them. The businessman seemed very pleased with them and was all smiles, telling her how well she painted and how the cards would sell easily. Barely able to contain her delight, she couldn't wait to show her parents the cards. They were impressed – she thought, well her mum was. Her dad seemed unconvinced that she had really painted the pictures that were on the cards. She didn't have the original images to prove it to him either. They were with the businessman.

Due to mutual friends and acquaintances, the artist and the businessman regularly met at certain events. She was surprised when, at one of those regular events, she met the businessman and he handed her some of the cards and asked her to pitch to local shops. Thinking this was a further venture into business in the art world, she agreed. Thankfully, a few local shop owners in Peckham were happy to host the colourful images in their establishments, grateful for the extra attention they attracted from passers-by.

For the most part, whenever the artist encountered the businessman at the meetings, they were cordial and he continued to encourage her. Enquiries about how business was going were met with enthusiastic replies at first. As time went by, a number of invoices were paid late and required gentle reminders by email or text. Eventually, some invoices remained unpaid, the businessman's greetings became less friendly, more stoic, he started to avoid conversation with her, choosing rather to exchange business-speak with his peers rather than an employee or contractor. He started to miss some of the meetings and eventually stopped attending those events altogether. Efforts to contact him by email and telephone were useless. He had cut her off. She asked people at the events if they had seen him. Yes, he was still in town and still doing business, just not with her anymore.

One day, out of desperation, she tried calling him. The student loan had run out completely. What was there to lose? She clicked on his number and put the phone to her ear, expecting the usual voicemail greeting inviting her to leave a message. To her surprise he answered! She barely knew what to say. His voice sounded cool, calm and collected, as usual, but she was sure she detected a hint of exasperation in his voice. Maybe he had deleted her number, forgotten it and answered the phone without looking at the screen first.

He must know he was wrong, that he had not treated her well by just disappearing from the scene with no explanation. She tried to stay as calm as his voice sounded, but a little heat began to rise in her. They exchanged small talk until there was an awkward silence and then she could not resist any longer. He owed her money for the paintings and she was not allowing this conversation to end without some commitment from him to pay.

"So erm... when do you think you will be able to pay for the paintings I sent you?"

"I've paid you for all the paintings you sent me, haven't I?"

She knew he was lying. He knew he was lying.

"No... there were a few on the last invoice that you haven't paid for."

"Well things have been a little slow you know, your cards are not selling like I thought they would. People are just not buying them." Was that her fault? She swallowed and thought quickly.

"Oh, I wonder why? Everyone I've shown them to has really liked them." Or were they just being polite? Now she wasn't so sure. "I'll check some of the shops that agreed to sell them and see how they're doing. Meanwhile, will you be able to pay that invoice?"

"Uh, yeah, I'll see what I can do," he seemed distracted.

"Ok… " Was that the commitment she had wanted? No! But she accepted it, for now.

"Alright then, I'll speak to you soon," he was suddenly in a hurry to end the conversation now and she had the distinct feeling it may have been the last time she would hear his voice for a while.

True to her word, the artist popped into a couple of the shops that had agreed to sell the cards. She felt proud to see them on prominent display as she walked in. She asked the proprietor how sales were going. The response was surprising and her smile would gradually disappear.

"Well, they haven't really been selling you know, people say they like the pictures but, you know black people, we like a lot of words and, well, there are not many words inside – just a couple. Like this one, just 'Happy Birthday', nothing else. They want a whole heap of sweet words, you know how we mout' cyan sweet."

The artist was shocked. She thought the pictures alone would sell the cards. She hadn't even thought about the inside contents but it was true, even she was persuaded to purchase cards based on the verse inside.

She left the shop quickly, refusing the offer to take them with her and "try somewhere else".

A range of emotions ran through her. First shock, then panic. She naively focused on the painting and left everything else to the businessman to deal with – she had not even thought about the words inside. She was good at writing. If he had asked her – if she had thought about it – she could have written some 'sweet mouth' words. Now she was annoyed with the businessman. He had claimed to have years of experience in this industry. He should have known that if he were targeting the African Caribbean community, they like sweet words and would not like cards with one or two words stating the obvious occasion. She was going to call him!

She did not rehearse what she was going to say. With the adrenalin coursing through her, she looked for his name and pressed the green call button. Again, surprisingly, he answered. She relayed the comments of the shopkeeper as calmly as she could and waited for his response.

"Yeah, with hindsight, I should have asked you if you could write the greeting inside too, but we ran out of time with the printer so I just wrote something quickly. Maybe we can use them again and this time you can write some nice words to go inside."

The artist was quickly losing confidence in him. Use them again? Maybe?

"OK, yeah I suppose so. So, do you know when you'll be able to pay me?" She was definitely not going to let him get away without a solid commitment to pay this time.

"Well you know, because the cards are not selling, I'm not sure you should expect me to pay you."

His words hit her like a ton of bricks. He had got to be kidding!?

"That was not the agreement. The agreement was you were paying me to use the images, not based on whether the cards sold or not." The heat was rising in her again. "And if you had got better words to put inside them, the cards would be selling!"

"Well that's not really how you do business you know. But OK, I'll see what I can do."

"No! You said that last time!" she realised that he had no intention of paying her.

"I want my money! You can't do that! I've got no money and I still have to go to university and pay my bills! When are you going to pay me my money!?" She was losing control, but she couldn't help it. He was trying to get away without paying her.

"Calm down, you need to calm down."

That was the worst thing anyone could ever say to her, especially when it was obvious that she would not be able to calm down for at least a week!

"Don't tell me to calm down! You owe me money that you agreed to pay and now you're trying to get out of it! Send me my money!" She lost it completely and started to sob. All her bills were floating around in her mind, especially her rent. She could lose her flat!

"I want my money! I want my money!"

"OK, OK, I see you're under a bit of pressure," he said, so calm she wished he was near her so she could smash the phone into his smug face. "I'll give you some time to calm down and I'll call you back."

She didn't wait to hear the click. Throwing the phone across the room, she curled up on her bed in a foetal position, stuffed the duvet into her mouth and wailed silently. She'd been had! She had been fooled by his sharp suits, expensive-smelling aftershave, top-of-the-range vehicle and, most of all, his silver tongue. And she didn't have a leg to stand on because there was nothing in writing about their agreement.

When she woke up hours later, the sky outside was dark and she was cold. She crawled under the duvet and went back to sleep. It wasn't worth being awake if there was nothing but depressing thoughts to deal with.

A few days later, the businessman did pay some of the money he owed. By then, she had started to put it out of her head, accepted that she had been very naive and the whole business 'deal' was over. She decided to just forget the whole affair and get on with her life. She eventually got a part-time job to supplement her student loan and life went on.

Life went on until she met another businessman and they got talking about her art degree and what she intended to do with it. He was slick! He knew the first businessman and claimed he would have been able to do more with her artwork than the first businessman had done. He convinced her to fight for what was hers. Furthermore, he convinced her to resurrect the dream and ask the first businessman to send her the original paintings. With renewed fire in her belly, she agreed. She had to ask someone for his number because she had deleted it from her phone and it turned out he had changed it from the one on his business card.

When she eventually contacted him, he was just as calm as ever. They exchanged the usual pleasantries and then she broached the subject of the paintings and asked if he had done anything with them. He hadn't. Good, she thought, he'll give them back to me if he's not using them.

"Well, I was thinking that if you were not using them, you could send them back to me."

"Well they are not yours any more, you know. Why do you want them back anyway?"

"I want to build up my portfolio. What do you mean they are not mine? Of course they are mine. You just paid me for the use of them – now you've finished and you're not using them any more, so you need to give them back." She could not believe what she was hearing.

"No that's not how it goes, you know. Once you gave them to me and I paid you, they're mine."

The artist felt the same heat, weakness and her breathing becoming rapid, just as in the last conversation she had had with him.

"They are my paintings. I let you use them and if you're not using them for the purpose that we agreed then you have to give them back."

"No, no, no," he was just as cool and laid back as ever. Now she wondered if his coolness was really some sort of disability. Maybe he didn't understand what she was saying. No one can be that cool in such a conflict!

"Yes, yes, yes! They are mine and you need to give them back! Now!" she was losing it again.

"No – you see… " he started to explain. She didn't allow him to finish. This time she would have the last say. "I'm taking you to court!" She shouted and ended the call triumphantly. It only took a few seconds for reality to set in and her conscience asked her the obvious question. How on earth would she even be able to afford to take him to court? Would a solicitor be interested in her little paintings on paper?

Over the next few weeks, she researched the law on artists' rights and ownership of art. It was complicated, extremely complicated. The worst thing was she had no written agreement. Disappointed, she decided to try another angle. She knew someone who the businessman looked up to, an older man. She would ask him to have a word.

She explained everything to him. He knew nothing about art and nothing about the deal, but she convinced him that the paintings did belong to her. He agreed to speak to the businessman on her behalf and ask him to return the paintings. Unfortunately, the businessman also capitalised on the ignorance of his superior and blinded him with science. He failed to get him to agree to return the paintings. In fact, he convinced him that she was in the wrong and the businessman didn't need to return the paintings.

The artist was disappointed and could not face another showdown with the businessman. It was over. She really needed to just kiss the paintings goodbye and move on with her life. Once again, she deleted his number from her phone and resolved to get on with her life. It was an experience she would learn from.

The final nail in the coffin came with a chance encounter at a meeting with a mutual friend, who informed the artist that the businessman had brokered the biggest deal of his life. He had sold the business. It transpired that the 'business' had been a small shop which doubled as his 'office' that he had referred to numerous times in conversation. He had sold the shop with all the contents – including her paintings – and migrated to the USA to seek his fortune over there.

The artist was almost grateful that the whole affair was finally, absolutely and completely over.

As the saying goes 'when one door closes another door opens'. As part of her dissertation for her degree course, the artist went on to meet some members of the upper echelons of UK society which saw commissions from various people, including an ITN news anchor and the mother of two famous Premier League football players. She was even head-hunted by an art promotion company to sell her work. This time, she ensured there was a robust contract in place.

As time went by, she completely forgot about the businessman and the disloyalty and exploitation she had endured. It had threatened to destroy her confidence in people, her studies and in the very industry she loved. But due to her faith in God, she was able to heal, learn from the experience and overcome without bitterness.

The artist moved into another industry and is now becoming known as an eagle-eyed proofreader. Using the wisdom gained from her previous experience, she is unlikely to be taken advantage of again.

The subject of the businessman never surfaced again until she was asked to be a co-author in the *Blind Spot* anthology with Sonia Poleon.

Windel Donaldson

Email: evangdon@gmail.com
Facebook: Windel Donaldson
Skype: EVANGDON

"Life Is A Narrow Path. Let's Fill It With Love."
Windel Donaldson

A preacher, singer/songwriter and an independent business owner, who loves to engage with like-minded people, Windel was raised by his grandmother, who was his rock. He left home at the age of 12 years of age and never looked back. He loves to travel and see the world.

Windel is a people person and loves to see everyone prosper in life, by helping them to dig deep down inside and pull out their God-given talents that are awaiting to enrich their life.

He has worked in many different establishments over the years and is loved by everyone who gets to know him.

In addition to all of this, Windel is a husband and father of five children.

Seeing The Unseen

It was around the beginning of March 1998, I came home one afternoon, had a shower and oiled my body. About four to five days before this, I would come home every evening from work, constantly playing this one song over and over again, 'Sin Doesn't Live Here Anymore' by Candi Staton.

On this particular evening, my cousin came to my house. He had asked to be dropped off by his brother, something he had not done before. He left his car at home and came to see me. I asked him why he'd come, he said he wasn't sure and felt that he should come and see me. I asked if he'd like a black coffee, knowing that's his favourite drink. I made him the coffee and said that I needed to pop to the bathroom, with no knowledge of what I needed the bathroom for. As soon as I got to the bathroom doorway, I felt as if there was a tap turned on at full power inside of me. I began to vigorously vomit pure blood, it continued for five to ten minutes. I knew at that moment, something was seriously wrong. My cousin was still downstairs in the front room, drinking his coffee, unaware of what was going on. My wife was already in bed by this time.

I shouted out, "I'm dying, I need to go to the hospital!" Suddenly I felt my body losing strength. I called my cousin and told him to take my car and drive me to the hospital. He came upstairs to see what was happening. He was shocked at the blood he saw all over the floor, immediately ran to get my car and move it to the front of the house, while I made my way to the front door.

The hospital was approximately three and a half miles away. It felt like the longest journey I had ever travelled. We waited over six hours in A&E. By this time, my eyes had gone dim and I could hardly see. I didn't even have enough strength to even talk to anyone. Despite this, I could hear my cousin constantly talking to me, "Cuz, are you OK? Are you OK?"

The biggest lesson I learnt while waiting all of that time in A&E is that your life could change suddenly at any time. My whole life flashed before my eyes, everything I did in my life, every single thing, up to that point. I learnt that, unless you have fulfilled what you were sent to do, life has no true meaning. Everything else seemed like a myth. I felt like 20, maybe 30 years had passed, but it had been just over six hours of me sitting there.

Finally, my name was called, my cousin helped me walk over to the doctor to be seen. I could still vaguely see. The doctor examined me and, as he did, he said, "I can't see why you have bled so much". I looked at him and said, "Doctor, I'm dying!"

I can remember clearly, while he was taking my blood, he looked straight into my eyes while he was doing it. Knowing there was a high awareness of AIDS and most doctors were cautious about procedures and protection against spreading the virus;, he didn't stop to think to put his gloves on. He panicked – I could see that he was scared in the way he moved from that moment.

While we waited for the blood results, I'm not sure if I died momentarily, but I remember being in a place between life and death. I had a feeling that I had failed God. It was a feeling of unworthiness, as if I was crossing over to another side. I gave up. I felt I wasn't worthy enough to live after this. I was ready to die.

Suddenly, a peace came over me. A peace so fulfilling that no money, woman or love could match it. I knew at this point that there was something beyond me. Something greater than anything I had ever known.

"Mr. Donaldson, we need to take you into Intensive Care so that we can remove all remaining blood. We believe it's poisoning your body." I heard this, but my eyes were still closed. Nothing else mattered because this feeling, this peace that I felt, was so real. I was transferred to Intensive Care.

They gave me blood straight away through a tube that was put in my neck. I heard them say that they needed to operate first thing in the morning, unless anything had changed by then.

After a few hours on the drip, I noticed the nurse that was assigned to me. She was from Malaysia. It seemed as if I was being checked often, maybe every 15 minutes. I could hear her asking if I was OK. I also heard her saying that she had a big party to go to. I wondered to myself why she'd be going to a party so late in the night. I must have nodded off after this.

When I was awoken, it was almost the break of day. The nurse who'd looked after me wasn't there, so I asked another nurse where she was, because I wanted to thank her for looking after me. She went to check the rota, but came back and told me she didn't know who the other nurse was.

The doctors came a few hours after that, with some students to check my notes. They said that the surgeon would come to see me in a while. I had tubes all over me, in my arms, neck and fingers and heart monitors on my chest and stomach. Finally, the surgeon came and checked my notes. He said, "Mr. Donaldson, your notes show that you remained stable throughout the night. We don't need to take you to theatre this morning. The nurses are going to continue to monitor your progress." They moved my bed into another room and just left me there. No nurse or doctor came to see me for a whole day. I thank God for the peace that came over me.

As I was lying there, my sister-in-law came to visit me. We spoke about the journey of life that she'd been through and a book she had read and lent me some years before. It was about the meaning of life. I shared with her the peace that I was experiencing and the need to have God directly in our lives. I was able to pray with her; she had not yet accepted the Lord as her saviour. As we shared the word of God, she wept and I knew then that God had given me a second chance to fulfil the mandate that was set before me.

I was in the hospital for quite a few weeks. I remember my wife and children coming to see me. I had two daughters at the time. My wife couldn't understand how all of this was happening to me. She was expecting our first son at the time.

Eight weeks later, I returned home from the hospital. It was made clear that there was an ulcer that had burst inside of my stomach. The doctors had put a camera inside of me during an earlier examination. I was given three boxes of medication to take home with me. I believe that something miraculous had happened to me on the first night in the hospital. This led me to not want to take the medication. I knew that I was healed from what happened on the inside.

I came home from the hospital. Everything seemed to be OK and my children were happy for me to be home. A day or two later, my wife and I went for a six-month check up for our child we were expecting. We were told that the baby wasn't getting enough oxygen from the placenta. The doctor prescribed aspirin to thin my wife's blood in hopes that it would help the placenta release oxygen.

After leaving the hospital, we went to my cousin's house, and he prayed, and prayed... and prayed. My wife opened up to me about the peace that she was unexpectedly feeling and that she didn't want to feel like she was ignoring the possible outcome. She just couldn't help this overwhelming feeling of peace that kept her calm.

We were booked for an appointment a week later to check if the aspirin had worked. They couldn't find our son's heartbeat. We were told our son had died; my wife remained calm.

The following Monday, we were due to go back to the hospital to be induced. My wife was given pethidine to start the labour process. After half an hour, he was stillborn in his sack, at just 4 lbs. 12 oz, on the 29th May 1998. My wife was given a word that explained the overwhelming peace, "There is a greater physician – God."

We made arrangements for his burial and had a church service to give thanks to God for he who knows all things best. God has since blessed us with three sons after this, two of them born in the same month, one being on the same date.

The most important things that I had learned throughout these blind spots was that I need support from my wife, friends and family. They were all there, without me asking. This has helped me to be more positive while in the face of adversity. Our church community was also very instrumental. Our assistant pastor at the time helped us to organise and carry out our daily tasks in preparation for the funeral, and visited us every single day while our bishop was away.

My wife had been a consistent support system throughout this time, despite her need for support and grieving time. She was never short of words of encouragement and the word of God. Through this, I was shown that, in trying times, we need each other to survive so that we can be the best that we were created to be.

It was in the same year, after my sickness, I experienced a financial downfall. After all of the previous years of savings, I now had no savings and no second income. I found myself in £21,000 of debt. Things were really tough and by now I had gone back to work. I was earning less than £12,000 a year. I had to consolidate all of my creditors into debt management and pay off the minimum payment over 25 years at £70 a month. The bailiffs had come and taken almost everything from our home, while I was at work, and demanded £3,000. My wife called me, as she was home alone; the bailiffs wanted immediate payment. I spoke with one of the officers and had no choice but to tell them to take what they needed. I would have paid prior to this if I had had the means to.

I was in Windsor Great Park when the Lord spoke to me clearly, "Speak to no one about this, go home, lock yourself in your room and glorify me, give thanks for all that's been happening in your life." I did as the Lord instructed.

The following day, while I was at work, my boss paid me £3,200. I collected my belongings and returned them to my home – all of which was unbeknown to me. He later made an agreement with me that I would pay him a small amount each month until I cleared the balance. A month later, I received a fax from him saying my debt had been written off and was paid in full. I believed that this was the end of everything.

Two weeks later, I opened a letter from our housing association. They were evicting us. Just a few weeks earlier, I had discussed our situation with our housing officer who had sympathised with us after learning that we had just lost our child and I was also very sick and forced to take time off work. Around four weeks had past and we went to court. The judge lifted the eviction notice and ordered us to pay our current rent, plus £2.50 per month.

As we walked out of the court, I saw a church sister of mine enter. She asked what I was doing at the court, I told her we were there for eviction. She said she'd visit in the week. Every month after this, she brought me £100 towards the rent arrears until the debt was paid off.

From here, it was an upward struggle to maintain my family and home. In the midst of it all, God always proved himself to be true to His word. As the song rightly said, "Great is thy faithfulness, morning by morning new mercies I see". There was always food on the table and clothes in abundance. All our needs were met. I was able to leave the position I was in at the time and become a director of that company. I then went on to start up my own business. I'm now a successful business owner.

Everyone meets their blind spot at some point in their life, but there is always hope if they continue to believe and trust in the help that God provides.

Sonia Poleon

www.sonia-poleon.com
Email: office@soniapoleon.com
Facebook: Sonia Poleon
Twitter: @SoniaPoleon
Instagram: @SoniaPoleon

*"The strongest oak tree of the forest is not the one that is
protected from the storm and hidden from the sun. It's the one
that stands in the open where it is compelled to struggle for its
existence against the winds and rains and the scorching sun."*
Napoleon Hill

Sonia is a successful entrepreneur, TV and radio show
host and award-winning author. She is also a mentor,
business and communications trainer, consultant and
inspirational speaker.

Sonia creates strategies, tools and tips that enable her
clients to overcome life and career struggles – shine like a
star and master their hustle.

Since 2002, Sonia has worked for herself. She's owned a
letting agency, transforming her first property into a profit
of a quarter of a million pounds. She has owned a successful

shoe shop and a children's nursery. These are all business experiences that she draws inspiration from.

"Every thought, idea, ambition that ever came into my mind, I'm going to achieve it. In order for you to have dreams, you have to dream."

In 2014, a guest appearance on local radio transformed into her latest endeavour – a talk show.

Sonia's talk show, Colourful Life, airs on Wednesdays, part of Colourful Radio's award-winning line-up. She's animated, passionate, excitable, self-driven, sassy and saucy.

Sonia's on-air chats are about culture and lifestyle, sandwiched between tunes – including spicy conversations with top-notch guests like Michelle Williams of Destiny's Child, Desiree Rogers (President Barack Obama's former Social Secretary), Levi Roots (a British-Jamaican reggae musician and entreneur), Lisa Nichols, and many more.

Not surprisingly, her sultry tone is often tapped for voiceovers, communications training and public speaking. Sonia also delivers nuggets of knowledge on her YouTube channel (Sonia Poleon).

When she's away from the microphone, Sonia mentors the next generation of disc jockeys through her Radio Rookie programme and helps those who are stuck to master their hustle.

"When people tell me they can't do X, Y, Z because of their kids, I tell them it's a load of rubbish. If I did it, you can do it!"

Held Hostage

Life is too varied and different these days. Gone are the days of people working in a factory when the worst job in the world seemed to be working for a shop called Woolworths.

As a teenager, my dream was to become a midwife. Back in the 1970s, in order to be a midwife, you had to be a State Registered Nurse (SRN) and all I wanted to do was deliver babies.

I wasn't a very studious person. I was very shy, not really confident, always sat at the back of the classroom, because I didn't want to be selected to do things.

In those days, the ethos was children should be seen and not heard, and so I made myself quiet in the classroom. I didn't want those teachers shouting at me the way they did at others, and I certainly didn't want to get the cane like the boys did in assembly in front of the whole year.

I remember once in junior school, I was in the playground with a friend, I put my hand round her neck and, in playing, I squeezed her neck too tight. She reported me to the head and I got a lash in the palm of my hand with the 12" ruler. That was enough to make me decide that corporal punishment was not for me.

I eventually went to secondary school, I was still shy in the classroom, but always managed to develop good friendships with others. Towards the end of school, I went to college to learn how to type, I found that I really enjoyed it and I became a very good typist.

Back in the 70s, when you left school, you had to go to a career officer who would look at your grades and tell you what occupation you should go into. I was devastated when they announced that I should go and be a typist because I really wanted to be a midwife.

I went home to tell my parents and, because they were law-abiding citizens and they believed that people in authority knew what they were speaking about, my parents advised me to go and become a typist. They thought I was going to get married, have children and stay at home. How wrong were they?

But yes, I went on to be a typist, and a very good one too! But I got bored easily, so after a while, I looked for my next challenge and so my working life grew. Then I found out about being a housing officer. A housing officer's job role was very similar to that of a social worker. I attempted to sign onto a course to become a social worker some time before, but was declined due to lack of qualifications.

So my quest was to become a housing officer. Wow, what a quest that was. It took me almost nine years to get a job in housing and, when I did, it was as a secretary in the development department. This is where they built all the properties. I learned a lot there, but I wasn't passionate about it. My husband would always tell me to stay there because that is where the money is, but I was more into job satisfaction than earning heaps of money. Yes, money is important, but I am motivated by much more.

I spent every possible moment speaking to housing officers and getting myself in trouble with my boss because I should have been doing my work. There were countless times I asked if I could get a transfer to the housing section and was always told 'no' - I should stay where I was. I requested to go on courses that would enable me to learn more about how the housing department operated and what housing officers did. I was told that I could only do courses that pertained to working in the development department.

So I embraced the development department, as there were some aspects of that job that I did like and that was selling houses. The government initiated two new schemes called Do It Yourself Shared Ownership (DIYSO) and Shared Ownership (SO).

This was it – I had found a passion for being in this department. It was my job to interview prospective candidates and show them the new properties we had for sale. I was fantastic at it. I was dealing with people, helping them to make one of the biggest decisions of their life (buying a home) and it was my project. When my boss saw how good I was, they arranged open evenings in show houses and it was my job to sell them like crazy. Every person that came to the development department wanting to enquire about purchasing through the DIYSO and SO scheme was sent to me.

But there was still that element of wanting to be a housing officer which always came back to me. I always applied for jobs outside the organisation, but I didn't have housing experience and it was difficult. Then the association I worked for had a temporary vacancy, I jumped at the chance and was given the job covering maternity leave.

When the previous housing officer came back from maternity leave, she asked me what I had done with her tenants. They had all formulated a signed petition saying they no longer wanted her to be their housing officer, they wanted Sonia Poleon. Needless to say, I was amazed and felt honoured, but managers could not possibly agree to giving a group of tenants what they wanted, even though I did a fantastic job.

I eventually got a housing officer job with another housing association. The patch I managed was a tough one. I had rough sleepers as tenants. These are people who live on the streets for long periods of time and then are given housing. They generally find it difficult to stay in one place, and at times, they give up their nice comfortable homes to go back to the streets. It was my job to ensure they engaged in life skills. I often helped find them day centres, colleges or jobs.

Then there were the people who just simply didn't like paying their rent, but they had all the mod cons, which often included massive flat-screen TVs that took up almost half the room. When you entered the living room, you felt like you were at the cinema. They just needed a good push to pay their rent, often a stern letter threatening to take them to court and asking the judge to give us back their home was enough to shake them.

Working in housing, we were always sent on short courses to learn how to take care of ourselves when on visits. Stuff like: ensure you sit next to the door, never take your shoes off, put all the lights on. I was experienced at this, because I had many occasions when tenants had been aggressive towards me due to them not being able to get their own way.

One tenant spent so much time hating me that she would ring and fill my mailbox with messages like, "You mixed up half breed," "I am going to have you beaten to a pulp," or "I am going to stick a piece of wood up your vagina and make it come out of your mouth." All because she wanted to move from a two-bedroom house to a one-bedroom flat with her daughter. I mean, who does that? She had a beautiful house and wanted to swap it for a flat she would only be overcrowded in and then want to move again, like she did before.

Over time, her threats got progressively worse and my boss didn't do anything about it. I asked him to come to the police station with me to report it. He looked up at me and said, "You can handle that," so off I went back to my desk and decided to forward his messages to the chief executive.

Needless to say, she took action straight away. She got on the phone to my boss and, next thing I knew, he was escorting me to the police station!

The police kept copies of the recordings, they went to her house and arrested her. She resisted arrest, but was eventually taken to the police station. The following months, she made it her duty to call me almost every single day, which made it worse. I kept copies of all her messages and, when I went to court and was in the witness box, her lawyers tried to cross examine me to make me out to be a liar, saying that it could have been anyone's voice, not his client's. I said,"Yes it could have been but, luckily for me, she gave me her name and address." She was so brazen, she tried to attack me in the courtroom.The judge was furious and she was given a nine-month prison sentence for harassment.

My blind spot really came when I was the housing officer for one tenant who seemed to be very nice. I was informed that he was a murderer, had just been released from prison after doing a 15-year sentence and was out on good behaviour.

One day he came to the office to speak with me. This was normal, as I was advised never to visit him in his home on my own. He was aware of this arrangement, so every time he came to the office, he would make an appointment. On this occasion, it seemed as though he had the world on his shoulders, things had not gone according to plan.

He had spent 15 years locked behind bars. Breakfast, lunch and dinner were cooked for him. All his utility bills were paid for, he might have lived on a minimum wage but, let's face it, there wasn't any chance of him going to the movies with his mates or even going to a nightclub. His only kind of recreation was with the other inmates and who knows how that was going. Either way, he was not coping well on the outside and I was going to know about it.

Imagine if the lock on his cell door had broke, how quickly it would have been fixed? If the glass in the window broke, how quickly would that have been replaced? If a knife or fork fell on the ground, my goodness, it would have been picked up pretty sharpish!

That kind of quick action was what he had become used to. If there was a problem, it would be solved straight away. The prison wardens were managing a lot of people at the same time, but it wasn't like that on the outside. If there is a problem, you report it and it is fixed in due course, not straight away.

Let's call him Mr. Harry. On coming to the office for his pre-arranged meeting with me, Mr. Harry was fuming. The receptionist called me pretty quickly, but they always did because everyone knew his past and were afraid - even my bosses, including the chief executive!

Over time, we had built up a rapport, so I wasn't scared. We went into the interview office, I asked how I could help him and he started listing all the things that had gone wrong in the flat; dripping tap, toilet not flushing, children had broken a window with their football and a few other things.

At first, I allowed him to shout and have his rant, but then it got too much and I got up to leave saying that, "I am not paid for you to abuse me, I am leaving."

Woah, who told me to do that? He told me, "Sit the fuck down and don't move because I am not finished with you yet." He went on to say, "Do you know that I have murdered someone before?" Before I could answer, he continued by saying, "I will murder again."

Of course, I sat my bum on the chair and just listened to him screaming and shouting. This went on for almost two hours. NO ONE came to my rescue, not a manager, not a colleague, no one. I was trained, so it was fine - yeah right!

I had never seen him like this before. The interview room we were in was a partition, so there were no brick or concrete walls that kept the sound out. The room was inside a large room where around five to seven people worked, therefore everyone could definitely hear him shouting at me. I was shocked and astounded, but I had to keep my cool. I opened my book, got out my pen and took copious notes so that he could see I was doing something. At times, I would ask him to slow down in order to write everything down. In asking him to slow down, I was literally trying to calm him down. It seemed to please him that I was taking notes, it showed him I was interested and doing something about his circumstances.

When he calmed down, I asked him if he would like a cup of tea or water. He told me I wasn't leaving the room until he had finished. I almost shat myself thinking where is back-up when I need it?! But through it all, I kept my calm.

It was at that moment I decided, this was not my life, I was no longer going to put myself in jeopardy and I was finished with housing. When Mr. Harry left the office, I spoke to the manager in the department in which the interview was located. I asked him why did he not come and rescue me. He responded saying he was listening and I was doing a good job, so he didn't want to disturb Mr. Harry's flow.

I went upstairs to my office and spoke to my manager, who also seemed to brush it off. So I reported this all to the chief executive, who also couldn't be bothered. It made me realise that to them, my life wasn't important.

Soon after, I handed my notice in to leave. Of course, they tried to make me stay which I did for a short while, but the urge to chase my dreams was far too strong, so eventually I left.

That was the beginning of my journey to the destiny I have created for my life today. Had that incident not happened,

I may still be working in housing and I would not be the compiler of this anthology.

The moral of the story is, every blind spot has its place in your life. Embrace it, thank it for happening and move on to the greatness that awaits you.

Everyone has a story

The stories in this book are just a few of the millions of stories of people all over the world. Your story is waiting to be told and someone is waiting to read your story and be impacted by it. Telling your story could catapult you into a whole new world, while encouraging others who may be going through a similar situation as you.

Here is an exciting opportunity for you to share your life experience. **Blind Spot Volume 2** offers the dynamic platform to tell your story with other like-minded people who recognise the power of telling their story in their own words. Are you ready to tell yours?

To take advantage of this once-in-a-lifetime opportunity, contact Sonia Poleon:

www.Sonia-poleon.com
Email: Office@soniapoleon.com
Facebook: Sonia Poleon
Twitter: @SoniaPoleon
Instagram: @SoniaPoleon